Children of Intercountry Adoptions in School

A Primer for Parents and Professionals

Ruth Lyn Meese

BERGIN & GARVEY
Westport, Connecticut • London

Library of Congress Cataloging-in-Publication Data

Meese, Ruth Lyn.
    Children of intercountry adoptions in school : a primer for parents and professionals /
Ruth Lyn Meese.
        p. cm.
    Includes bibliographical references (p.   ) and index.
    ISBN 0–89789–841–9 (alk. paper)
        1. Minority students—Education—United States—Handbooks, manuals, etc.
    2. Adopted children—Education—United States—Handbooks, manuals, etc.
    3. Intercountry adoption—United States.   I. Title.
    LC3731.M43   2002
    371.829—dc21   2002020849

British Library Cataloguing in Publication Data is available.

Library of Congress Catalog Card Number: 2002020849
ISBN: 0–89789–841–9

First published in 2002

Bergin & Garvey, 88 Post Road West, Westport, CT 06881
An imprint of Greenwood Publishing Group, Inc.
www.greenwood.com

Printed in the United States of America

The paper used in this book complies with the
Permanent Paper Standard issued by the National
Information Standards Organization (Z39.48–1984).

10 9 8 7 6 5 4 3 2 1

To my little "light," Katie Svetlana,
and
to my wonderful husband, Jim Windle,
Thank you. I love you both.

To the many courageous parents of intercountry adoption,
and
to the wonderfully caring teachers of our children,
I wish for you all the excitement and joy I have experienced.

Contents

Contents

Preface

In the 3-year period between 1997 and 1999, more than 45,000 children entered the United States as children of intercountry adoptions (INS, 2000), and over 18,000 more entered during calendar year 2000 alone. Approximately 60,000 others entered the country between 1990 and 1996 on daily "baby flights" from Romania, China, Korea, Guatemala, Russia, and the former Russian states (e.g., Latvia, Lithuania, and Ukraine). Compared to the waves of children adopted from Vietnam, Korea, or other countries in the 1950s through the 1980s, most of these "new" internationally adopted children were institutionalized in orphanages for 1 or more years prior to their placement in families. More than half of these children were 1 year of age or older at the time of their adoption. Research now indicates that some postinstitutionalized children experience significant learning and behavioral difficulties despite the love and care of their new parents, whereas many others display subtle difficulties posing problems for teachers upon school entry (Clauss & Baxter, 1997; Groze & Ileana, 1996; Price, 2000).

Parents are frequently ill-prepared to meet the sometimes overwhelming needs of their children and they are often at a loss regarding how to approach day-care providers or teachers regarding their child's adoption, birth country, and unique challenges. Teachers and other school personnel often do not understand the cognitive and emotional implications of institutionalization, nor do they recognize the socioemotional implications of adoption during routine classroom activities and social interchanges. Additionally, teachers and parents both may overlook the long-term difficulties posed by language differences or initial language delays years after the child appears "fluent" in English. These difficulties, which can be addressed when recognized, often go overlooked and result in faulty learning, frustration, failure, or inappropriate special education placements. For other children of intercountry adoption, lengthy institutionalization results in sensory deprivation, posttraumatic stress disorder, or a host of health and medical issues compounding language and cultural differences on school entry.

Nevertheless, children of intercountry adoption are unique individuals; some will do quite well and some will not. Children adopted internationally come to the United States from many different countries and widely different circumstances as infants, preschoolers, or older children. They come as the infant girl from China, the toddler boy from Honduras, or the school-age child from Russia or Romania. They come with their own unique backgrounds, personalities, and strengths, and they come to families offering them abundant warmth and love. Generalizations about these children are difficult to draw and parents and teachers may or may not "see" their child in this book. Much of the information contained herein comes from studies of the "new" child of international adoption currently entering the schools—the child who has lived in an institutional environment for much of his or her early life. *Although some of the information presented points to potential problems, this book is not meant to be a "gloom and doom" prediction of poor outcomes for all children of intercountry adoption. Rather, it attempts to present accurately what experts and parents currently know about these children as they enter school.*

This book, then, is intended for parents, teachers, and other school professionals such as special educators, guidance counselors, or social workers who must work together to meet the many needs of children of intercountry adoptions. In Part I, Understanding Children of Intercountry Adoption, I discuss the general health and development of children adopted from other countries, as well as the risks for later school performance associated with intercountry adoption. I also explore how adoption and institutionalization may affect children throughout the school years. In Part II, Helping the Child at School,

I first discuss how parents and teachers can work together to produce positive outcomes for these children in the classroom. Next, I examine relationships among language, learning, and limited English proficiency. Finally, I explain how parents and school personnel can access special education or Section 504 services for children when these are warranted.

Acknowledgments

A project of this magnitude would not be possible without the assistance of many individuals. I would like to offer my thanks to Lynn Taylor and Megan Peckman of Bergin & Garvey. Both Lynn and Megan provided valuable editorial advice and a genuine understanding of this subject. To Tyler Collins, my graduate assistant, who spent countless hours in the library and on-line locating references and resources and who constructed both appendices, Figure 1.1, and Table 2.1, I would also like to offer my sincere thank you. And, to Bridget McKeon and Dorian Tinaro, two additional graduate assistants, I owe my thanks for preparation of camera-ready artwork. To Crystal Thacker, I owe a thank you for hours spent creating the index. Finally, to the many parents who shared their experiences and "stories" with me, I would like to offer a humble thank you. We have a unique bond and a compelling mission.

Part I

Understanding Children of Intercountry Adoption

Chapter 1

Introduction: Who Are These Children?

Intercountry adoption, also called *international adoption*, refers to the adoption by U.S. citizens of children from other countries. According to Babb (1999), international adoption really began in the United States in 1955 following the adoption of eight children from Korea by Harry and Bertha Holt who later founded the Holt Adoption Agency, a national conference sponsored by the Child Welfare League, and congressional action. At the end of the Korean War in the 1950s and the Vietnam War in the 1970s, Americans adopted thousands of children either fathered by U.S. soldiers or left without families as a result of these conflicts. Intercountry adoptions declined in the 1980s, but shortly after the assassination in 1989 of Nicolae Ceausescu, the Romanian dictator, international adoptions by U.S. citizens once again increased dramatically. After seeing on their televisions hundreds of thousands of children shown living in horrendous conditions in huge orphanages throughout Romania, Americans traveled by the thousands to adopt their children (Bascom & McKelvey, 1997). As the former Soviet Union crumbled in the early 1990s, thousands more children in orphanages were adopted by U.S. parents, and adoptions of infant girls abandoned in the Peoples Republic of China have increased dramatically since 1994.

Babb and Laws (1997) estimated that intercountry adoptions comprise at least 10% of all adoptions in the United States. The actual percentage today, however, may be greater than that estimate. Increasing numbers of aging baby boomers seeking to establish or expand their families, couples faced with rising infertility rates, and a growing population of single individuals hoping to become parents all find a declining number of healthy infants available for adoption within the United States (Clark & Shute, 2001; Pertman, 2000). At the same time, socioeconomic and political disasters have resulted in numerous women around the world who are unable to care for their offspring and instead place their children in institutional care as "legal" orphans or wards of the state through abandonment. More than 600,000 children are currently orphans in Russia alone (*Russian Life,* 2001), and Evans (2000) reported that untold numbers of girls are simply "missing" from China's population through abandonment, abortion, and infanticide. Worldwide, many other children are simply abandoned to the streets or run away from institutional care to become "street children." As a result of these factors, intercountry adoption in the United States more than doubled during the decade of the 1990s, with most adopting parents having more education, higher incomes, and an older age than "typical" parents of young children (Groze & Ileana, 1996). Moreover, such a highly visible act as intercountry adoption has brought cultural and ethnic diversity to rural towns and schools throughout the country—everybody seems to know someone who has adopted internationally (Pertman, 2000).

In 1995, for example, Americans adopted 9,679 children from other countries. In 1996, they adopted 11,340 children, and in 1997, 13,620 adopted children entered the United States. According to the Immigration and Naturalization Service (INS, 2000), Russia and China currently are the most frequent destinations for parents hoping to adopt children. Of the children entering the United States with their new parents in 1997, 3,816 were from Russia and 3,597 were from China. In 1998, the number of orphan visas issued by the INS increased to 15,774 including 4,491 children from Russia and 4,206 from China and in 1999 the number increased once again to 16,396. For the year 2000 an additional 18,537 children, including 5,053 from China and 4,269 from Russia, entered the United States to join their new families. South Korea (1,794), Guatemala (1,511), and Romania (1,122) were additional countries from which large numbers of Americans adopted their children.

Approximately 64% of these children entering the country each year are female and 36% are male. Fewer than 50% each year are under the age of 1. In 1998, for example, 43% of the children from international adoptions were 1 to 4 years old, 8% were 5 to 9 years old, and 3% were over the age of 9. The INS reported similar statistics for 1997 as well (i.e., 41% from 1 to 4 years old, 11% from 5 to 9 years old, and 1% over age 9). If slightly more than 50% of the foreign-born children adopted by Americans are over the age of 1 at the time of their adoption, then we might expect at least 7,000 to 10,000 of these youngsters to be eligible to enter schools or day-care centers each year.

Approximately 40 children enter the United States with their new parents every day. Arriving from Russia or the former Russian republics such as Latvia, Lithuania, Bulgaria, and the Ukraine, or arriving from China, Korea, Romania, Guatemala, Vietnam, or one of several other countries, these children leave behind a language, a culture, and all that is familiar to them. Often, what is familiar to them is difficult for their parents and teachers to comprehend; daily life, sometimes for many years, in an orphanage or on the streets. Although Korea, Guatemala, and parts of Romania use a foster care system, about 80% of children currently adopted internationally, particularly those from Romania, Russia, the former Russian states, and China have spent 1 or more years in some form of institutionalized environment as illustrated in Figure 1.1 (Clauss & Baxter, 1997; Groze & Ileana, 1996; Price, 2000).

❋ LIFE IN THE ORPHANAGE ENVIRONMENT

Imagine yourself in a "baby home" or "children's home" in Russia. The year is 1996. You are 4 years old and have lived in this "home" since infancy. Your orphanage is among the "best" in Russia. You are asleep in one of 20 small beds, lined up head to toe in a room the size of most U.S. classrooms. You are suddenly awakened at about 6:30 A.M. by the lights ablaze overhead. The "mamas" enter, shooing you and the others still in underpants and t-shirts out of bed and into the bathroom. Everyone lines up on little green "potties" and then hurries to a designated chair in a larger adjacent room where an outfit, a sweatshirt and pants or maybe a dress and leggings, are laid out for each child. Your shoes have the ends cut out of them so that your toes can hang over the edge.

Your breakfast arrives at little tables in the same room where you found your clothing—hot kasha or gruel. You eat in silence and then

Figure 1.1
Percentages of Children of Intercountry Adoption from Orphanage and Other Systems (1995–2000)

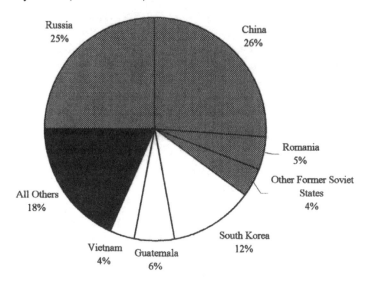

☒ Children from these countries come primarily from orphanage systems.

☐ Children from these countries are not primarily from orphanage systems.

■ Some of these countries also have orphanage systems, but do not provide a significant number of children.

line up to receive a drink. Donated toys line the walls in cabinets and murals decorate the walls, but you must tidy your living space before any play is permitted. Most children spend the day in the eating and living areas of this same room. You, however, are one of the "favorites" in the orphanage. You spend your day helping the "mamas" take care of younger children, some in large "crawling pens." You know how to scrub, clean, and help give injections. Lunch is placed on the little tables back in your age group's room, and again you eat in silence. This time you have a roll and an apple. You hold them one in each hand as you eat, as though fearful that someone else might get them. "Mamas" come and go on rotating shifts throughout the day and evening. You call each one by name, Mama Lyuda, Mama Nina, and so on. You rarely see a man. The day is regimented and structured. Children eat, drink, and use the bathroom in lines together. At day's end, you receive a small bottle of soured yogurt, called kefir, and curl back up in your little bed terrified of the woman with the big hands and tall boots who comes at night to scrub the toilets. You try not to think of her as you rock yourself to sleep.

You are in one of the "better" institutional environments. In other areas of the large concrete block building where you live, children considered "defective" (i.e., disabled) are housed out of sight in "lying down" rooms. These children may receive little stimulation or care from staff aside from being fed or changed. Many will die from disease and neglect, and others will linger into adulthood in similar institutions, retreating into themselves and suffering abuse from "caregivers" who may disregard cries for help or even dirty diapers for hours on end.

Children in Romanian orphanages in the early 1990s experienced similar treatment. Imagine yourself in a large building housing almost 1,000 children. All of the children are rocking in cribs in absolute silence. Bottles are propped on pillows for infants—there are too many children for caretakers to rock and feed individually. No one talks to you, sings to you, tickles you, or plays with you. In another area of the city is the Camin Spital, a large, cold institution for children considered "deficient." In these buildings, even children with minor, and often correctable, disabilities are warehoused, fighting for survival away from the public eye. Some children are tied to their beds or have their hands bound behind their backs to "protect" them from self-abuse. Others sit in their cribs surrounded by their own urine. Although Romanian officials insist that conditions have improved in state-run orphanages since the early 1990s, episodes of a *20/20* program aired on television in June 2001 vividly illustrate unchanged conditions for many Romanian orphans. In addition, "baby selling" for profit prompted a moratorium on Romanian adoptions in 2001 while government officials there contemplated changes in their adoption laws.

Similarly, children from China, most often infant girls, receive inadequate nutrition and stimulation. Bundled in many layers of clothing, imagine yourself, like many other babies around you, often spending hours on end in a crib. You are on a rigid schedule, a nap before noon, another nap in the afternoon, and 13 hours of sleep each night without feedings. Sometimes you have a crib mate, another baby girl placed in your crib by one of the "nannies" when beds are limited. You quickly learn to sleep with noise and people around you and your hands become your favorite plaything and source of comfort. You are barely able to pull your small body upright in the painted metal crib. You have a constant cold and develop a nasty cough and respiratory disease. Once you are potty trained, you become a helper for your caretakers—learning to accept and not question your "fate" in life (Evans, 2000).

Obviously, the quality and type of care given to children in institutional settings varies from country to country and even building to building. Sometimes, orphanages affiliated with particular adoption agencies become "showcases" for their countries and models for other orphanage directors as they benefit from an infusion of money and materials donated by adopting parents. Many other orphanages, however, particularly those in rural, difficult-to-reach areas of large countries such as Russia and China, remain desperately poor. Outsiders are still frequently denied access altogether to some orphanages as well as to certain areas of others (Evans, 2000; Pertman, 2000).

Nevertheless, awareness and thus the quality of care has improved somewhat since the early 1990s through the work of human rights and children's advocacy groups (Bascom & McKelvey, 1997). The United Nations, for example, in its 1989 Convention on the Rights of the Child, drafted several articles regarding intercountry adoptions and rights of children with disabilities. More recently, the Hague Convention of May 29, 1993 on the "protection of children and cooperation in respect of intercountry adoption" addressed the care of children and their rights during adoption. This treaty mandates a central authority in each country to oversee international adoptions and sets rigid standards for all agencies handling adoptions in Hague nations. Romania signed the document in 1994 and ratified it on May 1, 1995. Russia and China have also signed the document (September 7, 2000, and November 30, 2000, respectively), but fewer than 50 countries have accepted this multinational treaty to date. The U.S. House and Senate, however, approved the Hague Agreement in September 2000 and then-President Bill Clinton quickly signed the legislation that requires the United States to comply with basic human rights outlined in the Hague Convention regarding children adopted internationally including the following:

- To protect the rights of children and to prevent abuses against children, birth families, and adoptive parents involved in adoptions subject to the Convention and to ensure that such adoptions are in the best interest of the child; and,

- To improve the ability of the federal government to assist United States citizens seeking to adopt children from abroad and residents of other countries party to the Convention seeking to adopt children from the United States.

Moreover, as the central authority in this country, the U.S. Department of State is currently finalizing regulations for this law, the Intercountry Adoption Act of 2000 (PL106-279), and adoptive parent organizations such as Families for Russian and Ukrainian Adoption are offering input, particularly regarding advance training and receipt of complete medical information for prospective parents (FRUA, 2001). President Clinton also signed Public Law 106-395, the Child Citizenship Act of 2000, granting automatic citizenship, effective February 27, 2001, to children who are adopted by Americans abroad. Such highly publicized political activities served to heighten the awareness of most Americans regarding international adoption as a legitimate and rapidly growing way to form families.

Although conditions are improving for children in orphanages, these children are still experiencing institutional care with little similarity to life in a loving family. According to D. Johnson (2000), "an orphanage is a terrible place to raise an infant or young child. Lack of stimulation and consistent caregivers, suboptimal nutrition and physical/sexual abuse all conspire to delay and sometimes preclude normal development" (p. 6). In addition to poor nutrition and medical care, the following characteristics are often typical of the "best" institutional life:

1. Caregivers have little education or training and rotate in and out on shifts or stay for only a short period of time "on the job."
2. Children are abruptly transferred from one living area to another within the same building or from one orphanage to another within the city or region.
3. Children have limited meaningful language interactions with adults in order to extend vocabulary and sentence structure.
4. Daily life is regimented and lacks spontaneity (i.e., all activities including eating, sleeping, and using the bathroom may be expected of all children at the same time).

5. There is a lack of personal possessions, including clothing and toys.
6. Limited opportunities exist for exercise and development of gross and fine motor skills.
7. There is frequent exposure to infections through crowded living conditions, poor sanitation, and poor hygiene.
8. Children are exposed to environmental toxins such as lead.

Given the realities of institutionalized living, how do these children fare on adoption? Despite the conditions in which many children of intercountry adoption once lived, Groze and Ileana (1996) suggested there is much room for hope, but tempered with "cautious optimism" (p. 560). Let's turn now to an examination of the general health and development of children adopted from orphanages abroad.

GENERAL HEALTH AND DEVELOPMENT

Little is known regarding the long-term health and development of children of intercountry adoptions once they are home with their parents. Although early studies of children adopted from Korea point to successful home adjustment, school achievement, and racial identity (Simon & Altstein, 1991, 2000), such outcomes may or may not hold true for the "new" children of intercountry adoption from Romania, Russia, eastern Europe, or China. Several research studies, however, are now beginning to provide some information for parents and teachers. Obviously, generalizations can not be made and each child must be considered as an individual, but according to D. Johnson (2000):

> The chance of an institutionalized child being completely normal on arrival is essentially zero. . . . Kids aren't in orphanages because they come from loving, intact families with a good standard of living and ready access to good health and nutrition. Abandonment by a destitute, single parent with poor prenatal care and inadequate diet is the most common reason why a child is available for adoption. The second most common reason is termination of parental rights because of neglect and/or physical or sexual abuse (often alcohol related). Over 50% of institutionalized children in Eastern Europe are low birth weight infants, many were born prematurely, and some have been exposed to alcohol in utero. Finally, children with major medical problems or physical handicaps may be placed in orphanages by their parents due

to limited access to corrective treatment and rehabilitation services. These kids are a high-risk group by any standard. (p. 6)

Studies of Romanian Children

In one of the first evaluations of children in Romanian orphanages, Barbara Bascom (Bascom & McKelvey, 1997) examined 600 children. She found numerous health problems in these youngsters including the following:

1. Failure to thrive ("dystrophic" children) associated with low birth weight or with deprivation
2. Persistent small stature
3. Nutritional deficiencies
4. Communicable and/or infectious diseases
5. Chronic and recurrent middle ear infections
6. Birth defects
7. Musculoskeletal disorders
8. Strabismus and amblyopia
9. Lead- and radiation-related illnesses
10. Hearing impairments

Among the developmental disabilities noted were global developmental delays. As a matter of fact, Bascom reported that 85% of the children in her sample who had been in the orphanage for more than 6 months had some demonstrable delay. These children exhibited poor muscle tone (i.e., hypotonia), attachment disorders, behavior disorders, learning disabilities, profound delays in language and communication, posttraumatic stress disorder (PTSD), sensory integrative disorders, and lowered intelligence.

D. Johnson and his colleagues (D. Johnson et al., 1992) examined 65 adopted Romanian children, ranging in age from 6 weeks to 73 months, entering the United States in the early 1990s. About two-thirds of these children had spent their entire lives in orphanage care. They found only 15% of the children to be developmentally normal and physically healthy. Intestinal parasites and past or present evidence of Hepatitis B infection were noted in about half of the children. Most notable were patterns of growth failure associated with extended psychological harassment and emotional deprivation. As a matter of fact, Johnson found that children lose 1 month of linear growth for every 3 months they are in an orphanage, and he consid ered these children an extremely high-risk group.

In follow-up studies of 462 children adopted from Romania and living in the United States for 4 years or less, Groze and Ileana (1996) found that parents reported 60% of the children to be below normal weight and 49% below normal height at the time of their adoption. The majority of these children (93.5%) were under the age of 5 at the time of their adoption. Although most families reported no dif- ficulties with their children, 30.2% of the families noted language problems, 28.7% delayed fine motor skills, 25.7% delayed social skills, 23.8% chronic nonterminal medical problems, and 14.6% learning disabilities in their children. Seventy-five percent of the children in the survey were of school age. Of these, 25% ($n = 81$) were in special education classes for all or some of the day. Most of the parents (91%), however, viewed the child's adoption has having a very posi- tive or mostly positive impact on their family despite some behavioral difficulties such as wetting the bed or rocking.

Significantly, Groze and Ileana (1996) reported a relationship be- tween the length of time in an institution and delays in normal height and weight. Delays in fine and gross motor skills, social skills, and language skills were also related to length of institutionalization. Nev- ertheless, Groze and Ileana suggested that most of the children were developmentally appropriate and enjoying good relationships with their parents in a stable family. They cautioned, however, that a younger age at placement and the current status of the child were no guarantee that individual children would not develop special needs as they grew older.

Researchers from Great Britain and Canada, following children adopted from Romania by parents in those countries, found similar patterns of development and delays. Rutter (1998) and his colleagues, for example, suggested that children entering Great Britain before the age of 6 months were able to "catch up" in both physical growth and cognitive level by age four. Children entering after the age of 6 months also caught up; however, not as completely as the younger children, leading him to conclude that the strongest predictor of cog- nitive functioning at age 4 may be the child's age at the time of adoption.

The majority of adopted children (95%) entering British Columbia from Romania also exhibited developmental delays in three to four areas assessed including fine motor, adaptive, personal-social, gross motor, and language skills. Within 11 months, however, only 46% of the children still evidenced delays (Ames, Morison, Fisher, & Chisholm, 2000; Morison, Ames, & Chisholm, 1995). Length of time spent in the orphanage environment was highly related to lower developmental scores in all areas except motor skills, leading researchers to suggest that prospective parents should consider adopting the youngest child available. When children adopted from Romanian institutions after the age of 8 months were compared with same-age and same-gender children adopted in Romania before age 4 months and with never-adopted or institutionalized Canadian children, the children having stays longer than 8 months in the orphanage evidenced the greatest number of difficulties. On the other hand, Marcovitch, Cesaroni, Roberts, and Swanson (1995) agreed with Groze and Ileana (1996). They observed increasing difficulties over time for many children adopted from Romanian orphanages, even among the children who were youngest at the time of placement.

Studies of Children from Russia and Eastern Europe

Other studies have examined children adopted from Russia and the eastern European countries. Surveys conducted by adoption agencies, although containing some bias, suggest children from these orphanages adjust well on adoption. In a survey of 1,200 families sponsored by Cradle of Hope Adoption Center (1998), parents reported mild to moderate delays for their children on arrival in the United States. Severe delays were reported in physical development and expressive language for 21% and 22.5% of the children, respectively. After an average of 2 years home, however, 95% of the parents reported no delays or only mild delays for their children.

In a survey conducted by Rainbow House International, Clauss and Baxter (1997) received questionnaires completed by 206 families adopting children from Russia and eastern Europe. These children averaged 37 months of age at the time of adoption and had experienced an average length of stay of 30 months in the orphanage prior to their adoption. At the time of adoption, 73% of the families observed delays in their child's fine or gross motor skills, social skills, or speech and language skills. After an average of 23 months postadoption, only 39% of the parents reported ongoing delays. Of these, 32% reported speech and language delays, 13% reported fine motor skill delays, 13% reported social skill delays, and 10% reported gross motor skill delays. Another 10% of the children evidenced learning problems almost 2 years after their adoption. Additionally, a few children displayed behaviors considered problematic by their parents, including hyperactivity, aggression, "incessant chattering," and overly friendly or overly demanding and "clingy" tendencies.

Price (2000) surveyed 573 families having 798 children adopted from Russia (90.2%), Ukraine, Romania, Bulgaria, Kazakhstan, Georgia, Moldova, Belarus, Lithuania, and Latvia. These children ranged in age from 1 month to 14 years old at the time of their adoption and had been with their parents from 0 months to 8 years, 9 months. The average time spent in the orphanage for these children was 17.62 months (range 0 months to 11 years). Among her sample of children, the parents reported that 63.5% had experienced some form of physical or medical difficulty, one fifth had emotional problems including attachment disorder and attention deficit hyperactivity disorder (ADHD), and one fourth had developmental difficulties such as language or developmental delays. Interestingly, emotional difficulties did not surface until the children had been home an average of 3.67 years and had entered Grades 1 through 5 in school. Although Price found a relationship between the age of the child at the time of adoption and greater numbers of emotional problems, this relationship was very small. She also found many parents believed their children had special gifts and talents such as overall intellectual ability, music, and dance!

Albers, Johnson, Hostetter, Iverson, and Miller (1997) examined 56 children in international adoption clinics from June 1991 to March 1995. These children, adopted from Russia, Moldova, Ukraine, Albania, Kazakhstan, Latvia, Poland, and Bulgaria, were referred to the clinics by their parents shortly after their arrival in the United States. Like the children from Romania, these youngsters had growth delays—1 month of linear growth delay for every 5 months they had spent in the orphanage. Among the difficulties exhibited by these children were delays in fine motor (82%), gross motor (70%), language (59%), and socioemotional (53%) skills.

McGuinness (2000) also surveyed the parents of 105 children adopted from the former Soviet Union. These children averaged 7.7 years of age and had spent an average of 34.39 months in institutional care. She reported a history of alcohol abuse by the birth mother in the health information provided for 43 of these children. Although the majority of the children (85.4%) attended regular classrooms in their schools, two children were in a "developmental" kindergarten, one was in a special class for children with emotional and behavioral disorders, and five others attended a full-time special education class.

Studies of Children Adopted from China

Parents maintain that they adopt children from China because of the number of healthy infants available and the perceived lower risk of adopting a child exposed to alcohol, other substances, or HIV during pregnancy (Rojewski & Rojewski, 2001; Tessler, Gamache, & Liu, 1999). As a matter of fact, among 361 American families who responded to a survey conducted by Tessler and his colleagues about adopting children from China, 75% stated that the availability of healthy children was a "very important" factor in their decision to adopt from China. Also noted in the study were the relatively high education and income levels of these parents.

Nevertheless, for children adopted from China, some health and developmental difficulties are still apparent (Klatzkin, 1999). Miller and Hendrie (2000), for example, reported data on two groups comprising 452 children, primarily girls ($n = 443$), adopted from China. Of these children, 192 were seen at the International Adoption Clinic Floating Hospital for children between 1991 and 1998 and data for 260 others adopted between 1991 and 1996 were obtained through surveys of parents or physicians serving their families. Most of the children seen at the clinic had been home for only 2 months and ranged in age from 2 months to 12 years, 4 months at the time of placement.

Developmental delays were evident in 75% of the children seen at the clinic, including delays in gross motor (55%), fine motor (49%), language (43%), cognitive (32%), daily living (30%), and socioemotional (28%) skills. Growth delays of approximately 1 month of height age for every 2.86 months in the orphanage were also noted. Additionally, the two groups of children displayed similar numbers of medical problems including anemia (35%) and elevated lead levels (14%). Moreover, 18% of the children had hearing losses, orthopedic problems, or congenital anomalies not reported in the initial medical information received for them. Miller and Hendrie concluded that children adopted from China have medical difficulties and patterns of developmental and growth delays much like those of other children adopted internationally.

On the other hand, physicians from the International Adoption clinics at the University of Minnesota and Tufts New England Medical Center reported on the health status of 154 children adopted from China during a 36-month period (D. Johnson & Traister, 2001). The sample, primarily infant girls (98%), had been living in an orphanage for an average of 9 months. Among these children, infectious diseases were rare and blood lead levels were normal in most. For every 3.4 months the children spent in the orphanage, linear growth was delayed for 1 month; nevertheless, these physicians reported relatively few problems for children from China due to their limited exposure to institutional life.

Rojewski and Rojewski (2001) also found few delays among children adopted from China by 133 parents responding to developmental items on their on-line survey. Although they cautioned that parents electing to participate in the survey were asked to estimate whether or not a delay existed and the degree of severity of any perceived delays, 41.7% of the respondents maintained their child had no initial or current developmental delays. Of the 58.3% of parents stating their child had a delay in one or more areas of development on arrival, most indicated that their child had "caught up" by the time of the survey, approximately 2 years postadoption on average for these families. Twelve children, however, had no initial developmental delays but were perceived by their parents to have delays, particularly in language skills, from 3 months to 7 years after arrival home. Moreover, according to their parents, 46 children having initial delays continued to experience delays in one or more areas, although the children in this group were older at the time of adoption than the majority of the children in the survey.

Similarly, Bagley (1993) suggested that children adopted from China experience positive psychological and social adjustment and above average achievement in Great Britain's schools. Aronson (2001), too, characterized children adopted from China as hardy little youngsters. She cautioned, however, that many children experience respiratory problems, elevated blood lead levels, iodine deficiencies, intestinal parasites, developmental delays, and have unknown birth dates.

Summary of Adoption Outcome Studies

Given the somewhat conflicting results of these surveys, what can we say about the health and development of children adopted internationally? According to Melina (1995), most institutionalized children will display health and developmental difficulties to some degree on adoption. These children, however, also demonstrate significant progress after adoption. Although we do not yet know the extent to which initial problems exhibited by children adopted from orphanages can be overcome, we can make several generalizations:

1. Each child is a unique individual. Some children will adjust well and overcome initial delays. Others will not.

2. Children adopted from institutional environments are likely to exhibit delays in fine motor, gross motor, language, cognitive, and social skills. They are also likely to have medical and/or behavioral problems.

3. Adoption into a loving family and the provision of good nutrition are not enough to overcome months or years of deprivation. These children will require evaluation by trained professionals and some will require specialized interventions.

4. Length of stay and quality of care in the orphanage affect later growth and development. Neither a short length of stay or the "best" orphanage environment, however, can guarantee individual children will experience no difficulty on their adoption.

5. Children may experience "hidden" difficulties as they grow older, enter their school years, and advance up the grades.

❋ THE CHILDREN AND THEIR STORIES

According to Groze and Ileana (1996), some children of intercountry adoptions will have special needs that are immediately known. Others will evidence special needs on arrival home and evaluation by qualified professionals. For many others, however, unknown special needs may develop as they age, particularly as they enter school. Regardless of the age of the child at the time of placement, children of intercountry adoptions are considered by experts to be "high risk" (Bascom & McKelvey, 1997; Groze & Ileana, 1996; D. Johnson, 2000). Consider, for example, the difficulties posed by Jennifer and Laura on school entry and the unknown future of Olivia.

Jennifer

Jennifer was adopted at age 6 years, 4 months. She was among the many children rocking silently in a Romanian orphanage in the early 1990s. Jennifer was brought from the orphanage to her parents in a hotel room in Bucharest. She arrived in the United States in the spring of 1999. Her parents immediately enrolled her in a summer preschool to put her in contact with children of her own age. Jennifer's mother asked the local public school to test her immediately with the aid of a Romanian translator to see where she should be placed for the 1999–2000 school year. Jennifer did not perform well on the test given for kindergarten readiness, whether from lack of exposure to testing or concepts or from true delays. She could not name any colors, nor could she identify any animals in pictures. She could name very few body parts. The school recommended her placement in its half-day kindergarten program for the fall.

To Jennifer's mother it was obvious from the beginning that Jennifer had some major learning problems. It was November before she identified a single color correctly. She could name all of the colors in English, but it was over a year before she could consistently match the name of the color with the actual color. Jennifer was placed in the English as a second language (ESL) program at her school and received 40 minutes of instruction 4 days a week.

By January 2000, Jennifer's mother was very concerned with her progress. In addition to her difficulty naming the colors, Jennifer couldn't remember names, not even those of her best friends in school. Her mother asked to meet with professionals at Jennifer's school including the school psychologist, a nurse, the director of special education, a speech therapist, an ESL teacher, and Jennifer's kindergarten teacher. The team recommended a formal evaluation; however, the results were not particularly useful due to Jennifer's language difficulties. Although Jennifer functioned well in the school, her language had not developed sufficiently for the tests to be reliable. In a follow-up meeting, the team recommended a neurological evaluation to determine whether or not Jennifer's difficulties were due to a physical disability. In her state, international students are not eligible for special education until they have lived in the country for 1 year; nevertheless, the school's occupational therapist and physical therapist began working with Jennifer individually.

By the end of her first year in kindergarten and 1 year in the United States, Jennifer at age 7 could identify only about 6 letters of the alphabet (the letters in her name), could count no higher than 10, and could identify only the numerals 0 and 1. She still could not remember names nor could she identify shapes such as triangles, circles, squares, and rectangles. During the summer of 2000, a graduate student from a nearby university tutored Jennifer. In addition, she received weekly speech and language therapy through the local university.

In June 2000, a pediatric neurologist evaluated Jennifer. He diagnosed her with visual processing deficits, spatial and constructional skills and processing impairment, dysgraphia, impulse control disorder, social dyspraxia, and nondominant hemispheric dysfunction. In September 2000, the school team met again. Because of the neurological diagnosis, Jennifer now qualified for special education services and an Individualized Education Program (IEP) was developed for her (see Chapter 6). Jennifer was to repeat kindergarten and receive the special services designated in her IEP: (1) individual therapy from the speech and language therapist two times per week for 45 minutes; (2) individual help from the teacher consultant three times per week for 30 minutes; and, (3) individual instruction from the ESL teacher two times per week for 30 minutes. In addition, Jennifer was placed in an all-day kindergarten program for at-risk students, spending one-half day in the regular kindergarten class in the morning and then one-half day in a special class in the afternoon.

With all of the services that Jennifer received, she began making progress. Halfway through kindergarten for the second time, at age 8, Jennifer could now identify all the letters of the alphabet, both upper and lower case. She could count to 100 and identify numerals to 20. She now had no trouble remembering names and could identify all colors and shapes. She was even starting to read!

Her mother, however, remained concerned. Given the growth spurt Jennifer experienced on receiving improved nutrition and stimulation in her new home, her mother feared that a 9-year-old first grader might find it difficult to "fit in." In addition, Jennifer never talked about her life in Romania and never asked questions about her birth family. Her mother stated that Jennifer "behaves as if her life began at age 6 when she came to us."

Laura

Laura, the "favorite" child who rocked herself to sleep terrified of the woman who came at night to scrub the toilets, was adopted at age 4 years, 2 weeks, from Russia. She arrived in the United States in the spring of 1996. Laura's mother enrolled her in a summer preschool program, where she continued during the 1996–1997 school year. During this time, Laura learned English quickly and with little difficulty. In fact, by the end of the school year in the spring of 1997, Laura's mother met the parents of some of Laura's preschool friends They had no idea that Laura was not a native English speaker!

Laura began kindergarten in the fall of 1997 in the local public school. She attended a private kindergarten enrichment program in the afternoons. The school tested Laura for ESL and placed her in an ESL class 4 days per week for 40 minutes each day. Concerned that Laura would not be ready for first grade, her mother had several conferences with Laura's kindergarten teacher throughout the year to make sure that Laura was making good progress. By the end of kindergarten Laura still did not recognize all of the letters of the alphabet, but her teacher was not concerned. She indicated that she never considered having Laura repeat kindergarten and that Laura was a very popular child in her class who got along well with the other students.

Laura started struggling in first grade with both reading and mathematics. She was again enrolled in ESL classes, and again the school assured her mother that Laura would "catch up." Laura had difficulty sticking with tasks that were difficult for her and often just quit instead of continuing to try. By the end of first grade, Laura had started to read, but she was behind most of her classmates.

Laura was tested at the beginning of second grade. She was reading on an early first-grade level. She "passed" out of the ESL program by this time, but was placed in a special reading group in order to receive more individual help with reading. By the end of the fall, her mother was very concerned with her progress and started taking action, way too late as she now believes. Her mother had Laura tested at a reading center operating at a local university. Laura's intelligence tested as normal, but her language skills were very delayed, particularly her expressive language. Her reading tested at 1 year behind grade level. Laura's mother enrolled her in the reading center's Saturday school program in which children received 90 minutes of tutoring per week from a graduate student in the university's reading program. The tutoring appeared to help Laura and her mother continued with the same tutor throughout the summer. She also purchased workbooks to accompany the math books used in Laura's classroom at school in order to work on missing concepts at home. Unfortunately, the math program used by the local schools was almost totally language-based. Because Laura was still somewhat language-delayed, she had more trouble than most with this approach to math.

Laura recently completed the third grade. She was still struggling, but her mother believed that she was now at least "holding her own" and that she would advance to the fourth grade. Laura continued to participate in a special after school program where she received one-on-one tutoring in math for 30 minutes a day, 4 days per week. Additionally, she continued to attend the Saturday school at the local university. According to her mother, Laura's athletic prowess contributes to her self-esteem. She is quite athletic and enjoys participation in sports such as soccer. Sometimes, however, Laura cries and misses her "other" mother, particularly when she is very tired.

Olivia

Olivia, the infant girl sleeping 13 hours a night in her crib in China, was adopted in February 2001. At 16 months old, she weighed only 17 pounds and was barely able to stand with support. She was not walking, nor was she speaking any words. According to her mother, Olivia was very sick during her first month home. She had to be treated with a nebulizer every 4 hours and was almost hospitalized with a respiratory airway disease.

On arrival home, her mother was surprised that Olivia would sleep for such long hours at night without requiring feeding. She even slept in the presence of 21 rather noisy family members gathered for a family reunion! Olivia seemed to require adherence to a rigid schedule, napping both in the morning and in the afternoon regardless of noise or bright lights. Olivia's mother was also concerned with her baby's scratching. Olivia scratched anyone who came near her, so her mother tried to keep her fingernails trimmed. In addition, Olivia slept in an odd and uncomfortable-looking position, grabbing one wrist in her other hand, twisting it and pulling it up to her face.

After 5 months home, Olivia was generally healthy, smiling, walking, and speaking several English words. She now wore glasses to correct a vision problem her parents discovered as she turned 21 months old—severe myopia and an astigmatism. Olivia also now slept cuddling a blanket rather than her wrist. Her mother believes Olivia is one of the "lucky" babies adopted at the same time from her orphanage. She had the lowest blood lead level among the babies in her group, and her level has continued to drop. She also had a note written in Chinese for her parents to give her when she grew older. When Olivia was first found at a roadside and taken to her orphanage, pinned to her was the note written by her birthmother giving her exact birth date, time of birth, and the message "I hope someone kind finds her and I thank them all my life."

※ CONCLUSION

Children adopted internationally come to the United States from many different countries and many different circumstances. They come as infants, preschoolers, or older children—as baby girls from China, toddler boys from Honduras, or preschool or school-age children from Russia or Romania. Each has his or her unique background, personality, and strengths, and each comes to a family hoping to offer abundant warmth and love. Most of the recently adopted children in the United States, however, come to their families after months or years of life in institutions abroad.

Researchers and adoptive parents are only now beginning to understand the extent to which institutional life affects a child's development. Even children living in the "best" orphanage environment experience delays in growth, language, social, and motor skills. Many lack adequate nutrition and medical care, are susceptible to numerous infections, or have difficulty attaching to a caregiver. Of particular concern to parents and teachers, however, is how institutionalization will affect the child long term. Many of these children will develop normally on adoption and will do quite well in school. Although Victor Groze and others (Groze & Ileana, 1996; Price, 2000) suggest much cause for optimism, parents and teachers must understand the risks for school performance associated with intercountry adoption and work together to lessen the impact of these risk factors as these vulnerable children grow older.

Chapter 2

Risks for School Performance Associated with Intercountry Adoption

Do children who are adopted do as well in school as those who are raised by their biological parents? How do children who are adopted from other countries fare in school? Parents and teachers will find conflicting evidence and few certainties when searching for answers to these questions.

Some literature suggests that U.S. children who are adopted may be at greater risk than nonadopted agemates for school problems and special education placement (Bordwell, 1992). Silver (1989), for example, found that in a sample of students with learning disabilities, the frequency of adoption was 4.5 times greater than the norm. Brodzinsky and Steiger (1991), too, surveyed public and private schools and concluded that adopted children were overrepresented among children with neurological impairments, perceptual impairments, and emotional disturbances. On the other hand, children studied through the Colorado Adoption Project showed no signs of increased risk of learning disabilities or special education placement among "easily placed," Caucasian infants (Wadsworth, DeFries, & Fulker, 1993). According to Brodzinsky, Smith, and Brodzinsky (1998), the "vast majority of infant-placed adoptees do quite well and are within the normal range of psychological functioning" (p. 50).

Parents and teachers must certainly interpret the aforementioned research with great caution. Whether or not or exactly why children who are adopted are at increased risk of school difficulty and resulting special education placement is as yet unknown (Meese, 1999). Perhaps parents who adopt their children are more likely than biological parents to search for help or to "overreact" to small difficulties because they have gone to extraordinary lengths to have their children. Perhaps, they have become accustomed to using the services of various agencies (Deutsch et al., 1982). Or, perhaps children who later become eligible for adoption share a number of "risk factors" contributing to later "special needs" including a young birth mother, low birth weight, poor prenatal health care, alcohol or substance abuse by the birth mother, or early abuse/neglect (Silver, 1989).

In the United States, "special needs children" available for adoption are typically older children, sibling groups, and those with disabilities, although this definition does vary somewhat by individual states and various ethnic groups (Babb & Laws, 1997). Special needs children also include youngsters who are "at risk" for learning, physical, or behavioral disabilities in the future due to early abuse and neglect or prenatal exposure to alcohol or drugs (Babb & Laws, 1997). According to Brodzinsky et al. (1998), special needs children are more likely than those placed at infancy to have multiple adjustment problems and difficulties after adoption. Nevertheless, these authorities assert that most special needs adoptions are highly successful. Interestingly, in one large-scale study of 1,413 special needs children adopted within Oklahoma, Kansas, and Illinois, Rosenthal and Groze (1992) found positive results for almost 75% of the families responding to their survey, regardless of the child's age at the time of placement. Parental reports of aggression and "acting-out" behaviors were the only strong predictors of negative outcomes after adoption.

Today, many experts believe that *all* children of intercountry adoptions are at high risk and, therefore, should be included in the category of *special needs* adoptions (Babb & Laws, 1997; Bascom & McKelvey, 1997; Groze & Ileana, 1996). As increasing numbers of children of intercountry adoptions enter their school years, some may present obvious difficulties, and others more subtle learning and behavioral challenges to their parents and teachers (McGuinness, 2000). Particularly at risk may be those who have spent a significant portion of their early years in institutionalized environments.

❈ WHY INSTITUTIONALIZATION?

Difficult for many parents and teachers to understand is why so many children, even those who were most likely relatively healthy at birth, were placed in institutional care by the birth mother. Understanding the political, economic, and social forces resulting in such a placement may be intellectually easy, but emotionally difficult, for most Americans.

In China, for example, the Confucian philosophy of male dominance and families built on male lineage still persists, particularly in rural areas. Males usually inherit the family wealth and the responsibility of caring for aging parents, whereas females join their husband's family, even losing their place in their own family's records upon marriage. Thus, the "one child per family" policy in effect in many areas of this overcrowded country since 1979 favors the infant boy, who is seen as more "desirable" to the continuity and economic success of the family. So successful is this governmental "one child" mandate in China that boys now outnumber girls 117 to 100 (Beech, 2001).

In order to conceive and give birth in a hospital, for example, women had to possess a "birth permission paper" or *shengyu zheng* (Evans, 2000). Without this paper and "official approval," women who conceived more than one child could face sterilization, forced abortion, fines, or loss of housing and jobs, although couples having a girl as the first born were sometimes permitted a "second chance" to have a son. According to Evans (2000), many women who became pregnant without permission or after bearing a first child fled to cities or hid from officials, often giving birth in primitive conditions and becoming lost to their families. Sadly, social and political pressures to provide a male heir, cultural prohibitions against children born out of wedlock, and poverty often lead women whose first or "official" pregnancy resulted in an infant girl to abandon their child (Evans, 2000). Poor prenatal health care, the unavailability of good medical care, the practice of giving birth in the home, and famine brought on by natural disasters also increased the risk of premature or low birth weight babies born to these women.

The economic, political, and social forces leading to crowded Romanian orphanages are also thoroughly described in social work literature (Bascom & McKelvey, 1997; A. Johnson, Edwards, & Puwak, 1993; Pertman, 2000). In contrast to the stringent population control policy in China, under Ceausescu, abortion was outlawed, women under 45 were expected to have five children to expand the workforce, and participation in monthly "health checks" to determine or monitor pregnancy became mandatory for Romanian women. Families were relocated to small crowded apartments in cities, misguided agricultural policies resulted in food shortages, and health care was offered primarily to those who could work and, therefore, produce for the state. Doctors could be punished if children within their care died, thus the tendency was to place children in institutional or hospital care even for minor difficulties, further exacerbating health problems and often resulting in permanent institutionalization. Although conditions are now better in many Romanian orphanages than they were in the early 1990s, economic conditions still result in children being placed unnecessarily in institutional care. Moreover, some parents falsely believe that the orphanages have improved to the extent that their children may receive better food and medical assistance there than at home!

Elsewhere in eastern Europe, following the collapse of the Soviet Union, economic chaos drastically affected the lives of all, even those families who were secure under the Communist rule. Family members lost their jobs or suffered a reduction or loss of pay. Food and basic necessities became costly and difficult to obtain. Prenatal health care, birth control, and medical services were costly and inadequate. The rate of pregnancy increased in both younger and older women and alcohol abuse soared in all age groups (Aronson, 2000; Garrett, 1997). Women without the resources to care for one or more children abandoned their offspring to orphanages throughout Russia and the former Russian states.

China, Russia, and eastern European countries also lack the level of health and medical care for children we are accustomed to in the United States. According to Aronson (2001), even simple measurements of a child's height or weight may be inaccurate due to outdated, unbalanced scales or the practice of weighing children in China, for example, swaddled in many layers of clothing. Moreover, measurements of height, weight, or head and chest circumference may be taken by untrained staff or inaccurately recorded by translators during the preparation of documents for adoption. Accurate birth information is often completely unknown, and birth dates may even be assigned according to the date on which a child arrived in the orphanage.

Other cultural and societal differences interact with limited medical care to put children at risk for institutionalization. For example, Russia and eastern European countries view disabilities as less "curable" or "treatable" than we do in the United States. Children born prematurely, with low birth weight, or with minor physical or health problems are often considered "defective" and institutionalized along with those having more significant disabilities. These countries also use a system of medical diagnoses and classifications different than those used in the United States, which presents considerable confusion and concern to parents, physicians, and school personnel. In Russia and the former Russian states, pediatric training is limited and health care is based on a system of pathology, or a viewpoint that infants and toddlers are "neurologically impaired." That is, physicians often assign unusual, obscure diagnoses to infants during the first years of life, placing them at increased risk of institutionalization (Aronson, 2001). A further complication occurs when countries such as Russia are hesitant to permit the adoption of "healthy" children outside of its borders; therefore, physicians serving orphanages sometimes make diagnoses of unusual "syndromes" in order to permit certain children to be adopted internationally.

D. Johnson and Hostetter (2000), for example, found "perinatal encephalopathy" to be listed as the condition for almost all of the children from Russia referred to their clinic. In the United States, this term indicates a child at extremely high risk of mental retardation or cerebral palsy. In Russia, however, the terms *prenatal* or *perinatal encephalopathy* are frequently applied to children whose mother had some form of complication during pregnancy or child birth. Thus the physician might assign this diagnosis based on his or her subjective determination of poor prenatal health care, a maternal infection such as syphilis during pregnancy or prematurity or complications during delivery, including birth at home. In addition to pre- or perinatal encephalopathy, D. Johnson and Hostetter (2000) and Aronson (2001) listed the following diagnoses commonly seen in the medical records of children adopted from Russia or eastern Europe:

1. Pyramidal Insufficiency or Pyramidal Syndrome referring to delayed motor development or abnormal muscle tone possibly due to difficulty in the central nervous system, and myotonia or dystonia simply meaning abnormal muscle tone;
2. Hypotrophy, which when translated means "low growth";
3. Hypertension-Hydrocephalic Syndrome meaning an increased quantity of cerebrospinal fluid in the brain that may or may not require medical intervention;

4. Hyperexcitability Syndrome or Neuro-Reflex Excitability Syndrome referring to children who appear irritable and fussy, overactive, or with abnormal or "hyper" reflexes;

5. Delayed Speech and Language, the most common label applied to children of intercountry adoptions; and,

6. Oligophrenia meaning mental retardation.

D. Johnson and Hostetter (2000) cautioned that medical diagnoses such as these must be interpreted with extreme caution—*but never totally ignored*. For some children the initial diagnosis may have been accurate and may have resulted in the child's placement in an institution. For many others, however, after observation of the rate at which a child attains developmental milestones, the diagnosis becomes obviously inaccurate. The difficulty, of course, is that many of these diagnoses given to toddlers (e.g., delayed speech and language, low growth, poor muscle tone) are the *result* rather than the cause of institutionalization. Studies conducted as early as the first half of the twentieth century, for example, indicate that institutionalization negatively affects the growth and development of children (Spitz, 1945; Tizard & Joseph, 1970).

Parents can rely on pictures and videos to confirm obvious conditions, but they must seek help from physicians such as those at international adoption clinics (see Appendix A) having experience with children adopted from orphanages to confirm the accuracy of other diagnoses. For many other children, health and medical issues as well as cognitive and socioemotional problems that can potentially impact school performance may become apparent only on arrival home or careful evaluation by a physician (Hostetter, Iverson, Dole, & Johnson, 1989; D. Johnson & Hostetter, 1997). Parents and teachers must remember that children of intercountry adoption will probably vary as much as normally developing children and that they may, but most likely will not, be developmentally where their chronological-age peers are. Poor language stimulation, child-care practices such as swaddling in many layers of clothing, and limited opportunities for movement and exploration of the environment, for example, all may preclude development of cognitive, motor, and language skills at age-appropriate levels according to U.S. norms such as those listed in Table 2.1.

✳ HEALTH AND MEDICAL ISSUES

Numerous health and medical conditions may affect the child's growth and development and perhaps later school performance. Many of these, although easily corrected when the child is young (e.g., strabismus or "crossed" eyes), often go untreated and result in permanent debilitating conditions. Chief among the health and medical factors identified by physicians studying children at major international adoption clinics are Fetal Alcohol Syndrome and Fetal Alcohol Effects, exposure to various environmental toxins, infectious diseases, and impaired growth.

Fetal Alcohol Syndrome and Fetal Alcohol Effects

Fetal Alcohol Syndrome (FAS) may occur when the birth mother ingests alcohol during pregnancy. As alcohol is metabolized, it breaks down into substances toxic to the developing fetus. Alcohol also reduces the flow of blood, and thus oxygen, through the placenta. FAS is one of the leading preventable causes of mental retardation in the United States, having a worldwide incidence of approximately 2 children per 1,000 live births. In children adopted from Russia and the eastern European countries, however, the rate of fetal alcohol exposure may be much higher given the prevalence of alcohol abuse in these countries today.

Aronson (2000), for example, reported the rate may be as high as 15 children per 1,000 live births throughout the former Soviet Union. In the medical information received for 131 children from 1994 through 1997, she noted 17 containing indications of maternal alcohol abuse during pregnancy. Of these children, two met the criterion for FAS. Miller and Hendrie (2000), on the other hand, have not yet observed children with FAS among girls adopted from China.

In addition to mild to severe levels of mental retardation, FAS often results in poor muscle tone, poor coordination, behavioral problems, and ADHD (Mattson & Riley, 1997). Various congenital birth defects including visual problems (e.g., strabismus), skeletal deformities, cleft lip/palate, hearing loss, and/or heart and kidney problems may accompany FAS. Children with FAS typically have a characteristic appearance, tending to be small in size with a thin upper lip, flat philtrum, small cheeks and jaws, which give the face a "flattened" appearance, and small eye openings having folds of tissue in the corners. Aronson (2001) cautioned, however, that many children from

Table 2.1
Major Developmental Milestones

	Age	Cognitive	Physical/Motor
Infancy	Birth – 6 months	■ Realizes an object still exists when hidden (object permanence) ■ Recognizes familiar people, places, and objects ■ Increases attention	■ Rapid physical growth ■ Hearing and vision improve ■ Improves control of reflexes ■ Holds head up, rolls over, reaches for objects
	6 – 12 months	■ May find a hidden object ■ Improved recognition of people, places, and objects	■ Sits up, crawls, then walks ■ Grasps objects with thumb and forefinger ■ Imitates simple actions modeled by adults ■ Engages in purposeful activities
	12 – 18 months	■ Points to objects when named (body parts, pictures in books) ■ May find objects hidden in different places ■ Improved attention span	■ Continued, but slowed, growth ■ Improves walking ■ Develops more coordination and manipulation of small objects
	18 – 24 months	■ Demonstrates creativity and make-believe ■ Further development in memory abilities	■ Increased physical activity (runs, jumps, and climbs) ■ Further development in coordination and manipulation of small objects
	2 – 3 years	■ More complex and imaginative make-believe ■ Attempts to understand another's perspective ■ Differentiates between real and make-believe	■ Physical growth slows ■ Decreased appetite ■ Improves running, hopping, jumping, throwing, and catching ■ May eat with single utensil ■ Dresses and undresses self with some help

Stage	Age	Cognitive	Physical
Preschool	3 – 4 years	• Understands who, what, and where questions • Understands familiar cause-effect situations • Greater sustained attention • Can identify writing • May count small numbers of objects • Realizes there is a number order	• Can ride a tricycle, gallop, and skip • More coordinated running, throwing, and catching • May not require naps • Uses scissors with some precision • Scribbles, begins to draw "people"
Primary Grades	4 – 6 years	• Understands that letters represent sounds • May count forward or backward • Solves simple addition and subtraction problems • Stronger distinction between reality and make-believe	• Body's proportions are more similar to adults • Loses first baby tooth • Increased gross motor speed and endurance • Dresses self and ties own shoes • Drawings become more complex and accurate • Reads and writes own name
Primary Grades	6 – 9 years	• Consciously uses memory strategies to retain information • Develops more logical patterns of thinking • Mathematical skills increase in complexity	• More permanent teeth appear • Growth slows further • More legible printing and improved spelling • More detailed drawings with some depth cues
Upper Elementary	9 – 11 years	• Increased ability to plan and follow through • Utilizes more effective memory strategies • Increased size and organization of knowledge base	• Girls begin adolescent growth spurt • Athletic skills improve in speed and coordination • Drawings show further developments (depth and perspective)

Table 2.1 continued

Language	Social	Age
	Infancy	
• Reacts to loud noises • Listens to speech • Makes pleasure sounds and coos • Begins babbling and gurgling • Responds to "no" and changes in tone • Communicate wants through gestures	• Imitates facial expressions • Displays most basic emotions • Smiles and laughs	Birth - 6 months
• Responds to own name • Recognizes words for familiar objects • Uses non-crying sounds to get attention • Imitates speech sounds • Says words like "mama," "no," "bye-bye"	• Enjoys games like peek-a-boo • Responds to simple commands • Develops attachment to caregivers • May display separation and stranger anxiety	6 - 12 months
• Says first words • Listens to simple stories, songs, and rhymes	• Joins in play with familiar people • Displays some understanding of others' emotions (empathy) • Begins to follow turn-taking rules	12 - 18 months
• Vocabulary of about 200 words • Puts two words together to make sentences and questions • Uses words to influence others • Uses own name or pronoun (I, me) to label self	• Categorizes people by age and sex • Develops self-control • Recognizes goodness or badness of actions • Displays self-conscious emotions • Demonstrates gender-stereotyped choices	18 - 24 months
• Rapidly increasing vocabulary (has a word for almost everything) • Demonstrates developing grammar • Most speech is understandable to familiar listeners	• Develops self-concept and self-esteem • Understands patterns of cause and consequence • Distinguishes own acts as accidental or "on purpose"	2 - 3 years

	Preschool	Primary Grades		Upper Elementary
	3 - 4 years	4 - 6 years	6 - 9 years	9 - 11 years
	• Increased interest in playing with others • Develops friendships • Prefers playing with children of the same sex • Distinguishes others' acts as intentional or accidental	• Improved ability to interpret, predict, and influence others' emotional reactions • Understands and follows rules and behaviors based on a set of morals • Understands physical basis for gender	• Understands leader-follower relationships • Begins to compare self to others • Personal responsibility develops • Increased independence • Concept that justice is not based on equality • Better understands that people have different perspectives	• Connects success to ability, effort, and luck • Able to view self from another's perspective • Sophisticated sense of empathy • Trust becomes an important part of friendships
	• Talks to self during activities • Speaks easily • Speech understood by most listeners • Sentences often have four or more words • Adjusts speech to different listeners • Aware of some features of written language	• Vocabulary of about 10,000 words • Follows complex rules of grammar • Expresses empathy through language • Includes details in sentences • Correct pronunciation of sounds	• Continued rapidly increasing vocabulary • Concrete understanding of word definitions • Writing improves • Begins "reading to learn"	• Understands word relationships (synonyms, antonyms) • Grasps figurative language, double-meanings, and humor • Able to adapt communication to the listener • Masters conversational skills

Asia and Russia have this facial appearance as part of their ethnic heritage.

Children exposed to alcohol before birth may show some but not all of the characteristics of FAS. Often these children have no apparent abnormalities but experience Fetal Alcohol Effects (FAE), exhibiting behavioral and psychological manifestations as they age (Mattson & Riley, 1997). Children with FAE may have learning disabilities, attention deficits, poor impulse control, poor memory, and difficulty with cognitive and social skills required for success in school. Although FAS may not be evident in children adopted internationally, they are at risk for FAE if their birth histories contain evidence of maternal alcohol use. Children with either FAS or FAE require specialized intervention, often throughout the life span, to ameliorate the effects of maternal alcohol abuse (Spohr, Willms, & Steinhausen, 1993).

Exposure to Environmental Toxins

Developing nations throughout the world lack environmental protections like those existing in the United States. Thus, children born in those countries are at risk for exposure to various environmental toxins including radiation fallout, pesticides, and herbicides. Bascom and McKelvey (1997), for example, observed health problems related to lead, radiation (i.e., leukemia and congenital malformations from Chernobyl), and air/water pollution in Romanian orphans. Of particular concern is the exposure of Chinese children to lead through air and water pollution from coal burning, smelting factories, automobiles still using leaded gasoline, and lead dust coating food crops (Shen, Rosen, Guo, & Wu, 1996). Lead-based paints on toys, cribs, and walls, and lead solder used in old plumbing systems are two additional sources of lead poisoning.

Among 454 children adopted from China, Miller and Hendrie (2000) found elevated lead levels in 14%. Aronson (2001) also noted elevated lead levels in about 10 of the 50 Chinese children in her practice. In 1991, the Centers for Disease Control (CDC) recommended less than 10 micrograms per deciliter as the cutoff for acceptable blood lead levels. Aronson observed children with blood lead levels from 10 to 44, recommending a physician monitor them to determine whether or not the level declines.

Chelation therapy, a procedure used to rid the body of lead using Chemet or Succimer, oral preparations for reducing elevated blood lead levels, can be given to children with lead levels between 45 and 69, and lead levels above 70 are managed with medication and hospitalization. In a recent study of 780 inner-city 2-year-olds with lead levels from 20 to 44 per deciliter, however, Rogan et al. (2001) found treatment with Succimer/Chemet did not "undo" early damage by improving cognitive, psychological, or behavioral functioning at age 5.

For most children having lead poisoning, lead levels decline on removal from the toxic environment and/or on receiving treatment. Sustained exposure to lead, however, can damage the central nervous system; therefore, long-term effects of lead exposure may include difficulty with concentration, decreased appetite or activity level, and learning and behavioral problems when children enter school.

Infectious Diseases and Other Infections

Children crowded into institutions encounter unsanitary conditions and poor health care. Inadequate water treatment and poor sewage systems, for example, make water-borne illnesses and intestinal parasites prevalent among children in institutions, and caretakers can expose children to various communicable diseases such as tuberculosis. In addition, malnourished, neglected children often have weakened immune systems, making them even more vulnerable to infection (Dorfman, 1999).

Among 52 children adopted from Korea, India, Central or South America, the Philippines, and Taiwan, unsuspected cases of Hepatitis B, cytomegalovirus, tuberculosis, and intestinal parasites were diagnosed by physicians at the International Adoption Clinic at the University of Minnesota (Hostetter et al., 1989). Miller and Hendrie (2000) reported Hepatitis B, Hepatitis C, intestinal parasites, tuberculosis, and congenital syphilis among children adopted from China. Hepatitis B, Hepatitis C, tuberculosis, intestinal parasites, and cytomegalovirus have also been reported for children adopted from Romania, Russia, and eastern European countries (Aronson, 2001; Bascom & McKelvey, 1997; D. Johnson & Hostetter, 2000; D. Johnson et al., 1992).

Like children in schools, children in orphanages are also susceptible to numerous respiratory and ear infections. Chronic or recurrent otitis media (middle ear infections) are frequently reported for institutionalized children (Bascom & McKelvey, 1997). These infections are often left untreated, however, causing rupture of the eardrum and permanent mild to moderate levels of hearing loss as well as associated language delays.

Hepatitis B, intestinal parasites, and repeated infections pose long-term health risks for children including liver damage, hearing loss, reduced growth and development, and failure to thrive. D. Johnson and Hostetter (1997, 2000) and their colleagues recommend all children arriving in the United States through intercountry adoption receive the following screening tests as part of their postarrival evaluation:

- Hepatitis B profile including HbsAG, anti-HBs, and anti-HBc
- HIV-1 and HIV-2 testing by ELISA for children over 18 months of age and by ELISA and PCR culture in children less than 18 months
- Mantoux (intradermal PPD) skin test for tuberculosis with Candida control to control for reduced immune system activity
- Stool examination for ova and parasites
- RPR or VDRL for syphilis
- Complete blood count with erythrocyte indices
- Dipstick urinalysis
- A developmental exam, particularly for those who have been institutionalized
- Lead level and antibodies to Hepatitis C for children from eastern Europe, Russia, and China
- Hypothyroidism for children from China (due to high incidence of dietary iodine deficiency)
- Vision and hearing exams. (D. Johnson & Hostetter, 2000, pp. 18–19)

Impaired Growth

Missing information about a child's birth (e.g., birthdate, length of gestation, length and weight at birth) or about the height of his or her birth parents makes predictions regarding the child's future physical growth difficult. Too, some racial differences in final height and weight exist that must be considered when predicting a child's growth pattern. Moreover, some growth lags seen in children from intercountry adoptions may be culturally induced. Children in Asia, for example, may have underdeveloped muscles from swaddling or from being carried. They catch up quickly, however, once they are given the opportunity to use their leg muscles! Nevertheless, growth delays are common in children adopted from orphanage environments. Delays in height and weight may be due to nutritional factors or to psychosocial factors.

Growth delays related to poor nutrition are more evident in a child's reduced weight than in his or her height (D. Johnson & Hostetter, 2000) and often are a result of improper infant formula or poor orphanage diet. Children lacking adequate nutrition may have "floppy" muscle tone, poor teeth, or "bowed" legs. According to Aronson (1998), calcium, iron, and vitamin D are often lacking in the diets of children in institutional care, affecting bone and muscle growth and strength. Moreover, rickets, a bone and muscle disease resulting from vitamin D and calcium deficiency, has been observed in children adopted from Romania (Bascom & McKelvey, 1997), Russia, and the other eastern European countries (Albers et al., 1997), and China (Miller & Hendrie, 2000). For many other children, malnutrition, with associated growth failure and irritability, is a result of easily transmitted intestinal parasites that prevent proper absorption of nutrients by the body, such as *Giardia lamblia*, common to children living in orphanages. Fortunately, with aggressive treatment of parasites and malnutrition, children can overcome much of the growth delay caused by pre- and postnatal nutritional deficiencies (Aronson, 2001), although the long-term affects of malnutrition on a child's neurological and cognitive development may not be evident until the child grows older (Dorfman, 1999, 2001).

Of equal importance are psychosocial growth delays, which affect height more than weight. According to D. Johnson and Hostetter (2000), children experiencing psychosocial growth delays typically lose one month of linear growth for every 3 to 4 months they have been in an orphanage. These delays are related to the lack of attention and stimulation and to the emotional deprivation experienced by children living in crowded institutions—conditions inhibiting the body's production of growth hormones (Bascom & McKelvey, 1997). Federici (1998), for example, described children he believed to be 5 or 6 years old, but who were really in their early to mid-teen years, among those he observed in Romanian orphanages. Children with psychosocial delays often have poor motor skills and they may also exhibit unusual behaviors such as head banging and sleep disorders.

As with nutritional growth failure, children with psychosocial growth delays frequently do respond well and grow quickly when given abundant attention and stimulation. Many, however, still experience long-term delays in stature as well as in motor, cognitive, and social skills (Rutter, 1998). For others, with attention, stimulation, and improved nutrition, comes precocious puberty resulting in embarrassment and social consequences for an already vulnerable youngster (Melina, 1998).

▧ COGNITIVE AND SOCIOEMOTIONAL ISSUES

Related to nutritional and psychosocial growth delays are numerous cognitive, social, and emotional effects of orphanage life. Research indicates that the developing brain is quite "plastic," yet critical periods in the first few years of life do exist for healthy cognitive growth, particularly for language and emotional development (Bowlby, 1988; Locke, 1993). Unfortunately, malnourished children experience lethargy, decreased muscle tone, and poor balance and coordination, making them less likely to explore their environment or to seek social stimulation during critical developmental periods. Faulty heating systems in cold institutions can also restrict exploration of the environment and interaction among toddlers. Most importantly, however, children in institutions may receive little attention or stimulation from their caregivers.

In many orphanages, for example, children like Jennifer discussed in Chapter 1 are confined to cots, cribs, or playpens, or to a single room. Absent are the mobiles, toys, and playthings that encourage children to reach out, crawl, walk, interact, and explore their environment. Caregivers, although they may be kindly and well meaning, simply may not have the time to pick up, hug, or play with the children. Children may be fed in their cribs through bottles propped on pillows or they may be fed thickened mixtures through bottles, alone in their cribs, for so long that they can not tolerate the texture of solid foods or the touch of other human beings. These children do not have the opportunities to be touched, rocked, cuddled, and talked to during feedings—important activities for bonding, socialization, and language development. Lacking are important experiences such as having books read aloud, going on trips to the store, and engaging in conversations with adults who can answer questions. Sadly, meaningful language stimulation during the first 2 years of life is extremely limited for many children in orphanages, a cognitive deficit that may never be overcome (Gindis, 2000).

According to Ames et al. (2000), many children who were older than 2 when adopted from Romanian orphanages have cognitive deficits. They found that these children had lower intellectual ability when compared to Romanian children who were adopted at a younger age or to Canadian-born children. They suggested that the children who had lengthier stays in the orphanage environment fell further and further behind their peers and thus had less time to make up for lost experiences prior to entering school. Children adopted at age 4, like Laura for example, had only 1 or 2 years to make up for 4 years of "lost" experiences necessary for social, language, and concept learning before being judged against their agemates in school.

Too, as children are moved from one institution to another with increasing age or as caregivers or other children rotate in and out, children lack consistency in relationships with those around them. They lack the opportunity for gazing into a mother's eyes as she feeds them, rocks them, and talks to them. They lack the consistency, safety, and security of one constant caregiver. Some resourceful children such as Laura learn to seek attention from others around them. These may become the "favorites" among orphanage caregivers and receive more preferential treatment, and thus more stimulation, than others (Morison et al., 1995). Children who are weakened by hunger or illness and those with lower cognitive ability may be less fortunate and receive reduced attention. Some children, deprived of almost all human contact and affection, turn inward to a world where hand flapping, body rocking, and "infant babbling" provide some degree of pleasure and the only source of communication. Federici (1998) terms this syndrome *Institutional Autism.*

Socioemotional, cognitive, and language delays have been noted among children from Romania, Russia, eastern Europe, and Asia. In children from Romania, for example, Groze and Ileana (1996) found a relationship between institutional placement and behaviors such as rocking, hitting oneself, being over- or underreactive, and being scared or anxious and inconsolable when upset. Similarly, Marcovitch et al. (1995) reported temper tantrums, inability to pay attention, high activity level, overfriendliness, anxiousness, and distractibility among adopted Romanian children, although many of the behavioral difficulties parents initially reported decreased over time. Children adopted from Russia, the former Soviet states, and China also exhibited developmental delays in language, cognitive, and socioemotional skills (Albers et al., 1997; Miller & Hendrie, 2000; Rojewski & Rojewski, 2001).

Price (2000), too, noted attachment disorder and ADHD among children adopted from Russia and the former Soviet Union. She also suggested a relationship between being a "favorite" in the orphanage and emotional problems. That is, children whose parents identified them as having been a "favorite" in the orphanage were rated as having fewer emotional problems than those who were not judged to be a "favorite." Price also found age to be the greatest predictor of emotional problems among these children, although children who were older at the time of adoption had only slightly more emotional issues than children who were younger.

With the help of consistent, caring parents some children from institutionalized environments can and do "catch up" to their peers socially, emotionally, and cognitively after adoption (Price, 2000; Rojewski & Rojewski, 2001; Rutter, 1998). McGuinness (2000), for example, reported that parents and teachers judged the majority in her sample of 105 children to be socially competent with few conduct problems. She suggested that cohesion and expression of feelings led to a family environment ameliorating, to some degree, the risks of previous institutional living. Many children, however, will exhibit long-term developmental delays in cognitive, language, and socioemotional skills requiring intervention once they enter school. Although delayed language is the most frequent developmental delay reported for children of intercountry adoption, language is so vital to cognitive and school performance that language issues are addressed separately in Chapter 5. For now, among the most perplexing socioemotional problems for parents and teachers noted for children from orphanages are posttraumatic stress disorder (PTSD), sensory integrative problems, and attachment disorders.

PTSD

PTSD was first identified in "battle-fatigued" soldiers returning home from war. The sudden, horrific shock of witnessing death or disaster was a traumatic event in the lives of these individuals resulting in their feelings of helplessness and terror. Originally thought to be a temporary condition, the long-term effects of repeated exposure to trauma received publicity and scrutiny when many veterans of the Vietnam War experienced continued sleep disturbances, flashbacks, and behavioral changes in the months and years following their arrival home.

Unfortunately, PTSD can affect children as well as adults. When children experience the sudden death of a parent or the devastation of war or natural disasters, they too may suffer long-term consequences. According to Maskew (1999), the effects of such trauma in children include the following:

- Sleep and toileting disturbances
- Hypervigilance
- Startle responses to loud or unusual noises
- Behavioral and mood changes
- Repeated telling of events
- Reenactment of events in play
- Separation anxiety
- Flashbacks to the event, often in response to sensory triggers such as smells, sights, or noises
- Avoidance behaviors. (p. 226)

Almost certainly children of intercountry adoption experience some form of trauma placing them at risk for PTSD. The death of parents, abuse and neglect in the home, and economic, political, or natural disasters most likely result in their abandonment to an orphanage in the first place, and for many prolonged trauma continues following their institutionalization. Rotating shifts of caregivers, children arriving and departing, limited stimulation, neglect, and even daily abuse are insidious events conspiring to prevent feelings of safety and security. Instead, repeated traumas such as these produce constant stress, fear, and a sense of helplessness that may not be overcome even when the child moves to a stable and loving home environment.

Of particular concern is recent research indicating the effects of abuse and neglect on socioemotional development. Pollak, Cicchetti, Hornung, and Reed (2000), for example, demonstrated a relationship between abuse and neglect and a child's ability to recognize facial expressions. When compared to peers, neglected children make fewer distinctions between expressions such as happiness and sadness, whereas physically abused children perceive even neutral facial expressions as angry ones. These researchers hypothesize that neglected children receive fewer emotional learning opportunities when they are young and that abused children receive more hostile ones. Both groups of children, however, later experience difficulty accurately recognizing and responding to social signals of peers, parents, and teachers. Thus, these children might respond to the sad, neutral, or even happy facial expressions of others inappropriately and as if these individuals held malevolent intent. Obviously, such inappropriate responses might result in confusion or angry reactions from their recipients.

Similarly, Martin Teicher (2000) and his colleagues described permanent changes in the brains of children who are psychologically abused. According to Teicher, early abuse results in a "cascade of effects, including changes in hormones and neurotransmitters that mediate development of vulnerable brain regions" (p. 54) and that predispose "the child to have a biological basis for fear . . . [and] to be more irritable, impulsive, suspicious, and prone to be swamped by fight-or-flight reactions that the rational mind may be unable to control" (p. 65). In short, Teicher suggested that children experiencing early abuse and neglect may have a brain "wired" to be negative in its response to stress and that they may be at increased risk for behaviors associated with PTSD.

Specifically, Teicher described the following manifestations in the brain as a result of repeated psychological abuse and neglect in childhood:

• Limbic irritability—The child evidences EEG abnormalities much like temporal lobe epilepsy and may appear "spacey" and "dreamy" or aggressive and irritable.

• Deficient development of the left hemisphere and faulty left-right hemisphere integration—The left hemisphere of the child's brain, as well as the corpus collosum, are smaller. Adults with PTSD use their left hemisphere to process neutral situations but switch to the right hemisphere when faced with stressful events or memories. So, too, do children who are abused and neglected. Under stress, these children abandon the logic of the left, verbal side of the brain and react through the right hemisphere where emotions and memories of early trauma are stored. The two hemispheres are less likely to communicate and balance the child's responses to stressful situations.

• Increased activity in the cerebellar vermis—This area of the brain regulates emotion and attention and has a large number of receptors for stress hormones. Early trauma appears to impair the ability of the cerebellar vermis to maintain emotional balance.

Interestingly, Teicher (2000) suggested that decreased maternal attention in young children can predispose the child to have heightened levels of fear and negative reactions. Neglect decreases the production of thyroid hormone, which then results in a decrease in serotonin in the hippocampus (i.e., an area of the brain in the temporal lobe involved in memory and emotion) and reduced development of receptors for various stress hormones. Thus, the inadequate development of stress hormone receptors increases the child's risk of stress hormone responses during disturbing events. High levels of stress hormone also inhibit the development of the cerebral cortex and the left hemisphere of the brain during the critical time of language development from ages 2 to 10. The child's brain essentially becomes programmed to be hypervigilant, constantly on guard against danger, and less rational and logical at times of stress.

Such traumatized children might regress and respond like a younger child when under stress. Seven- or 8-year-old children might, for example, scream and cry with anxiety like toddlers when their mothers are unexpectedly out of sight. Or, these children might jump or flinch when someone makes a rapid motion toward them. Likewise, traumatized children might misunderstand facial expressions and enter a "survival mode" when they are upset or confused. Teachers and parents are unlikely to reach these children through talk and logic at these times. Rather, they must provide signs of calm and safety until the child regains his or her emotional control.

Sensory Integrative Problems

Ayres (1979) suggested that early sensory stimulation is essential to a child's healthy development. Children must process not only sensations received from vision and hearing, but also those from touch, body position, and body movement. These various sensory inputs must be analyzed, organized, and integrated by the brain in order to develop the perceptual and self-regulatory skills necessary for later success at play and at school (Kranowitz, 1998). When the brain cannot integrate the sensory information it receives, children cannot respond and behave in an organized and consistent manner. According to Ayres, the first year of a child's life is crucial to proper sensory integration.

Children raised at home are picked up, bounced, rocked, and tickled by parents and other caregivers. They have soft blankets and toys to touch and manipulate, and they are given foods of increasingly complex textures and tastes. All of these activities stimulate both the tactile (touch) and vestibular (movement and balance) systems. Children become accustomed to touch, to the feel of various textures, and to movement. Initially when they are moved, reflexes allow infants to adjust their head or body position automatically, but as babies gain experience with movement these reflexes gradually disappear. The child is able to crawl, walk, run, balance, and further explore the sights, sounds, tastes, and textures of the environment. According to Kranowitz (1998), by the time children enter preschool, they have typically achieved a number of complex sensory skills including the following:

- The ability to modulate touch sensations through the skin, especially un- expected light touch, and to discriminate among the physical properties of objects by touching them (tactile sense)
- The ability to adjust one's body to changes in gravity and body position, and to feel comfortable moving through space (vestibular sense)
- The ability to be aware of one's body parts, and to move one's muscles and limbs in a coordinated way (proprioceptive sense)
- The ability to use the two sides of the body in a cooperative manner (bilateral coordination)
- The ability to interact successfully with the physical environment; to plan, organize, and carry out a sequence of unfamiliar actions; and to do what one needs to do (praxis). (p. 49)

Infants raised in orphanages may not have received these sensory inputs during early critical periods of development. Unable to explore the environment and seldom touched, picked up, or rocked by care-givers, the child may respond with fright or defensiveness when moved. Other children deprived of sensory stimulation may seek "self-stimulation" through habitual behaviors such as rocking, further reducing their ability to interact with their environment. Groze and Ileana (1996), Bascom and McKelvey (1997), and Cermak and Daunhauer (1997), for example, all report both sensory and tactile defensiveness among children from Romanian orphanages.

Children with sensory defensiveness may not like to be physically active or they may become distracted easily by sounds (Cermak & Daunhauer, 1997). Conversely, they may tune out activity around them and be difficult to engage or they may have trouble shifting focus from one activity to another. They have difficulty regulating their responses to sensory stimulation, overreacting with fear when picked up by caregivers, or alternatively running and jumping until exhausted. These children may have trouble concentrating in school with distractions surrounding them. Children having sensory integra-tive difficulty may also avoid movement and games other children enjoy such as swinging, sliding, climbing, jumping, and running on the playground (Haradon, 2000).

Children with tactile defensiveness may find the texture of shirts or pants or the labels inside of clothing to be extremely uncomfortable. Towels may feel overly rough, a bump in a sock may seem worse than a rock, and light caresses from parents may be unbearable (Melina, 1995). They may be picky about the texture of foods, gagging when fed unfamiliar meals. Some children may perceive touch to be dangerous, avoiding contact with or standing too close to others, or choosing quiet playmates not likely to jostle and push (Haradon, 2000). Children with tactile defensiveness also may not like getting dirty or engaging in activities like finger painting and water or sandbox play.

According to Ayres (1979), some children with tactile defensiveness overreact to the slightest touch as if it were painful. Some push others away or react to touch with aggression. Some children have trouble sensing touch, not registering light touches, or requiring shoelaces to be tied overly tight. Still others become annoying to parents, teachers, and peers by incessantly touching others or their belongings (Haradon, 2000).

Certainly not all children of intercountry adoptions will experience sensory integrative difficulties. Those having sensory processing problems, however, may have trouble with typical school tasks such as manipulating a pencil to form letters, cutting with scissors, staying within the lines to color or write, tying shoelaces, or following a sequence of instructions. Other signs of sensory integrative difficulty include frequent irritability, constant motion such as rocking, excitability in crowded places, anxiousness in new situations, and a strong need for preparation in advance before changing from one activity or plan to another. Fortunately, occupational therapists can provide sensory integration training to improve a child's success in the classroom. Too, parents and teachers can take steps such as the following to help children with sensory integrative difficulty explore touch and movement at their own pace:

- Carefully observe the child's reactions to sounds, touch, and movement as well as the types of sensations the child appears to be seeking.
- Refrain from forcing the child to participate in activities (e.g., bear hugs, swinging, spinning) causing signs of distress.
- Provide opportunities for the child to engage in activities under his or her own initiative (e.g., finger painting, writing in pudding or Jell-O, playing

with sand or dry beans or rice, riding on low tire swings or tricycles, rolling on floor mats, hiding under pillows or blankets, jumping through hula hoops placed flat on the floor).

- Remember that the child may need to concentrate when attempting difficult tasks, so he or she may not be able to listen and talk while swinging or jumping, for example.

Sensory and tactile defensiveness can certainly also affect the later development of positive interpersonal relationships with parents, teachers, and peers. Teachers, for example, may easily misunderstand unusual reactions to touch or problems tuning out background noise, believing these to be behavioral problems. In addition, children who cannot color, cut with scissors, or properly form their letters may fall quickly behind in school. Furthermore, self-esteem and social acceptance can suffer when children are clumsy, awkward, uncoordinated, and fearful compared to peers. Most importantly, the child with sensory and tactile defensiveness unfortunately may be at increased risk for successful attachment to his or her parents. When children who experience tactile or sensory defensiveness are touched or moved, they may respond with fear, screaming, flinching, or struggling to be free. The child's parents may be shocked and surprised by this behavior. They may become hurt, frustrated, or even angry as the child they worked so hard and long to adopt appears to reject them. The process of bonding and attachment is at risk of disruption.

Attachment Disorders

Bowlby (1988) and Ainsworth (1982) suggested that infants engage in numerous interactions with their mothers essential for forming loving, secure, trusting relationships with others later. Bowlby, for example, suggested that crying, smiling, clinging, and following are survival behaviors of infants that evoke maternal responses (Karen, 1998). Thus, mothers and fathers attuned to their babies quickly respond by feeding, diapering, holding, smiling, and talking when infants need their attention. The infant responds by gazing at mother or father, smiling, and receiving their attention joyfully. Through these many positive responses from a consistent caregiver to fulfill the infant's needs, the child begins the process of healthy emotional development. Mother becomes the source of love and affection and the secure base from which the toddler begins to explore his or her environment. The bond of attachment between mother and child is firmly established.

As a matter of fact, Ainsworth (1982) described three patterns of attachment behavior among children. *Securely attached* children are those who look for mother when they are upset. They are confident that mother will be available and they accept her comfort easily. Some children exhibit difficulty with attachment, however. The *avoidantly attached* child, for example, seems to avoid or not to care about mother. This child may be "clingy" or demanding and aggressive with mother, but unable to accept comfort from her when upset. Finally, the *ambivalently attached* child is also clingy and demanding, but is anxious and seeks comfort from mother, although the child is difficult to soothe. Although Ainsworth's (1982) descriptions of attachment behaviors among children continue to be highly debated, her work has served as a foundation for studying children for whom the normal process of attachment was disrupted.

When infants are raised in overcrowded institutions, for example, caregivers are unable to respond immediately to their needs. No one comes when they cry, when they are hungry, or when they are hurt. Moreover, as caregivers come and go on rotating shifts, these children lack the consistency needed to form a safe, trusting relationship with one individual to whom the children are special. Over time, as basic needs for physical contact, food, and warmth are not consistently met, these children develop other ways—manipulation, screaming, "charm"—to make people satisfy their needs (Hughes, 1998, 1999). Children who fail to feel special and safe and to bond to one caregiver are at risk to develop an attachment disorder.

Children with attachment disorders may resist comfort by adults, create barriers to closeness with others, and push those around them away by their actions. These children may be "hypervigilant" and watchful, evidence a heightened startle response, or demonstrate increased irritability, anxiety, hyperactivity, and regressive behaviors (James, 1994). Sometimes, these children act "old for their age," preferring to engage in activities typical of older children and to take charge of younger children. When these youngsters are met with limits on their behavior, however, they may revert to the actions of the young child—having temper tantrums. Conversely, many children with attachment disorders are overly friendly to everyone, treating strangers as if they were relatives and forming only superficial friendships with peers.

The American Psychiatric Association (1994) lists the criteria for reactive attachment disorder of infancy or early childhood in its *Diagnostic and Statistical Manual of Mental Disorders (DSM-IV).* Among the markers are the following:

A. Disturbed and developmentally inappropriate social relatedness in most contexts beginning before age 5 as evidenced by either (1) or (2)

1. Inhibited Type—Persistent failure to initiate or respond in a developmentally appropriate fashion in most social interactions, as manifest by excessively inhibited, hypervigilant, or highly ambivalent and contradictory responses (e.g., a mixture of approach, avoidance, and resistance to comforting, or frozen watchfulness)

2. Disinhibited Type—Diffuse attachments as manifest by indiscriminate sociability with marked inability to exhibit appropriate selective attachments (e.g., excessive familiarity with relative strangers or lack of selectivity in choice of attachment figures)

B. The disturbance is not accounted for solely by developmental delay (as in Mental Retardation) and does not meet criteria for a Pervasive Developmental Disorder (e.g., as in Autism Disorders)

C. There is a presumption that the disturbed behavior is due to persistent disregard of the child's basic emotional (e.g., for comfort, stimulation, and affection) and physical needs and/or repeated changes of primary caregiver that prevent formation of stable attachments. (adapted from p. 118)

Dissatisfied with the vague *DSM-IV* description of attachment disorder, Hughes (1997) developed a list of characteristics frequently observed in children with attachment difficulty. When children persistently exhibit these "symptoms" despite consistent caregiving and a healthy psychological environment, Hughes asserted poor attachment may be suspected. These symptoms include the following:

• A compulsive need to control others, including caregivers, teachers, and other children
• Intense lying even when caught
• Poor response to discipline—becoming aggressive or oppositional-defiant with ordinary discipline
• Lack of comfort with eye contact
• Problems with physical contact—wanting too much or too little
• Lack of mutual enjoyment and spontaneity in interactions

• Disturbances in body functioning (e.g., eating, sleeping, urinating, defecating)
• Discomfort and resistance with increased attachment
• Indiscriminate friendliness—charming, easily replaced relationships
• Poor communication with many nonsense questions and much chatter
• Difficulty learning cause and effect and poor planning/problem-solving skills
• Lack of empathy with little evidence of guilt or remorse for others
• Ability to see only the extremes—believes situations are all good or all bad
• Habitual dissociation or habitual hypervigilance
• Pervasive shame with extreme difficulty reestablishing a bond after conflict. (adapted from p. 30)

Are children from intercountry adoptions, particularly those adopted from institutions, more at risk than peers for attachment disorders? Behaviors associated with attachment disorders have been reported in most studies of children adopted from orphanages in Romania, Russia, and the former Soviet states (Chisholm, 1998; Clauss & Baxter, 1997; Groze & Ileana, 1996; Marcovitch et al., 1995; O'Connor & Rutter, 2000; Price, 2000). The percentage of parents reporting these difficulties was relatively small in each study, however, with the indiscriminately friendly behaviors predominant in most children reported to have attachment problems (Chisholm, Carter, Ames, & Morison, 1995).

Interestingly, Chisholm and her colleagues suggested that indiscriminate friendliness might actually be an adaptive behavior on the part of children raised in Romanian institutions. That is, normally developing infants easily interact socially with unfamiliar adults between 2 to 7 months of age, until they become more attached to their primary caregiver and more cautious around others by approximately 9 months of age. Because children in orphanages do not have multiple experiences with one special caregiver, Chisholm speculated that much like the infant some children learn to be friendly and loving toward everyone who responds to them. Furthermore, she suggested that parents may not view these overly friendly behaviors as problems until they begin to worry about their child's safety or grow disappointed that their child treats them in the same manner as a stranger.

Similarly, Groza (cited in Keck & Kupecky, 1995) maintained that children in institutions learn tolerance, distance, and routine rather than love and affection. Although they may learn the value of belonging to a group, they often lack the sense of trust on an individual level. They may also become passive and fail to develop cause-and-effect thinking—learning through multiple experiences, for example, that crying or attempts at attention have no results or that feeding and other routines occur not when needed but rather on a schedule.

The exact relationship between institutionalization, deprivation, and attachment disorders is unknown. O'Connor and Rutter (2000) found, for example, an overall relationship between the duration of deprivation and attachment disturbances, but surprisingly 70% of the children in their sample of children adopted from Romania did not exhibit marked or severe attachment difficulty despite profound deprivation of more than 2 years. Additionally, some children evidenced attachment disturbance even when they experienced deprivation only in the first months of life. Thus, O'Connor and Rutter suggested that early deprivation might have long-term effects on attachment, but that grossly poor care is not a sufficient condition for an attachment disorder to develop.

Zeanah (2000), too, suggested that children adopted from orphanages have an increased risk for attachment difficulty. He maintained that the inhibited/withdrawn reactive attachment disorder is very rare, but that many children continue to exhibit the indiscriminately friendly type of behaviors long after adoption and attachment to their parents. He also asserted that accounts sensationalized by the media of poorly attached postinstitutionalized children who are violent, explosive, and aggressive with only the primary caregiver are inconsistent with the *DSM-IV* criteria for reactive attachment disorder that requires the behaviors be seen across several settings. Therefore, Zeanah believes that the *DSM-IV* criteria may not be adequate for describing the disorder as evidenced by some postinstitutionalized children, or conversely that these children may simply be erroneously labeled as having a reactive attachment disorder.

Similarly, Federici (2000) asserted that older children who have lived in institutionalized environments for more than 2 to 3 years may be exhibiting signs of PTSD and are inappropriately labeled as having an attachment disorder. As a matter of fact, he suggested that children adopted over the ages of 3 or 4 are likely to appear moody, depressed, irritable, angry, and frustrated as they encounter new people, a new culture, a new language, and new demands. They are overwhelmed, overstimulated, and highly anxious.

On the other hand, Rojewski and Rojewski (2001) argue that very few children adopted from China exhibit any signs of attachment difficulty. As a matter of fact, the child who cries and initially resists his or her new parents in China may indeed be demonstrating the effects of early positive attachment to caregivers and the potential for later attachment to his or her parents. Rojewski and Rojewski suggest that early age at the time of adoption, Confucian ethics valuing child care, and the older age and more stable socioeconomic status of many parents choosing to adopt from China are but a few of the reasons why attachment problems are infrequent among Chinese adoptees.

Nevertheless, Chisholm (1998) and O'Connor and Rutter (2000) suggested a modest relationship between behaviors associated with attachment disorder and parent or teacher reports of emotional disturbance, inattention, hyperactivity, and externalizing (i.e., acting out or disruptive) behaviors. Although the long-term implications of attachment difficulties exhibited by children of intercountry adoptions are as yet unknown, Hughes (1998, 1999, 2000) stated parents and teachers may encounter the following:

- Manipulation—Child pits parent against parent or parent against teacher
- Resistance to traditional forms of behavior management—Concrete rewards such as stickers have no lasting value; time out is seen as a rejection or as an opportunity to avoid the "annoying" adult; and privileges are lost as a way to demonstrate hate and "get back at" parents and teachers
- Strong battles for control—Because the child constantly strives for control, parents and teachers may have to keep the child "off balance" by shifting approaches to discipline rather than by adhering to a consistent plan.

As a matter of fact, Hughes (2000) suggested parents and teachers should relate to the child with an attachment disorder like they would to a much younger child. Jewett Jarratt (1994) and Keck and Kupecky (1995), too, suggested that older children who are adopted may need time to regress and be treated like a young child. These authors maintained that these children need nurturing and structuring activities congruent with their emotional, rather than chronological, ages. Smiling, laughing, talking, singing, and playing "pat-a-cake" games provide opportunities for nurturing experiences, for example. Playing games requiring turn-taking or mirroring behaviors and reading to these children while sitting close are two additional ways for parents and teachers to give safe "nurturing" experiences. Limiting choices throughout the day also provides the structuring necessary to demonstrate to these children that they are living in a safe environment concerned with their best interests.

Experts have developed several interventions for children with attachment disorders. Some of these involve confrontational techniques such as restraint or "therapeutic holding" and are quite controversial (see, e.g., Cline, 1992; Federici, 1998; Welch, 1988). More acceptable to most parents and school personnel, however, are interventions based on play such as "Theraplay" (Jernberg, 1979). Data regarding the effectiveness of each of these interventions, however, is limited.

※ THE CHILD IN SCHOOL

Children who are ready for school persist at challenging tasks, have good language development, can communicate well, listen, and pay attention. Reports from the National Institute of Mental Health (NIMH), however, are now pointing toward factors placing children at risk for academic and behavioral problems in school (Huffman, Mehlinger, & Kerivan, 2000). Among the risk factors identified by the NIMH reports are cognitive deficits, early behavioral problems, problematic parenting practices, and difficulty establishing early relationships with important others such as parents, peers, and teachers. According to Huffman and her colleagues, socioemotional readiness is at least as important as academic readiness for successful school performance. Although the NIMH reports are primarily applicable to "typical" children raised in the United States, many children of intercountry adoptions may well be at risk for successful school outcomes given the cognitive and socioemotional deficits imposed by prior institutionalized or otherwise inadequate care.

Of particular concern, too, are recent reports examining the nature of child care experienced by children in the United States. Children who are in high-quality day-care settings (e.g., low adult–child ratio, educated staff) for the first 4½ years of life score higher on tests of language and cognitive skills than do children in lower quality day care (NIH, 2001). However, children who spend more than 30 hours per week in day care are rated as more aggressive in kindergarten than are children spending less time in day care. These results are disturbing given the implication that consistent caregiving—especially that of a mother providing attentive care to her children at home—is important for the social relationships necessary for early school success.

Children of intercountry adoptions often come from institutional environments, environments probably far less adequate than those of most day-care arrangements in the United States. Even the best institutional environments lack the nutritional, medical, physical, cognitive, and social stimulation essential for healthy growth and development. Too, children in the best institutional care abroad come to their new homes lacking the language skills and concepts typically attained by American preschoolers. Although most children from intercountry adoptions do very well on arrival home, the long-term effects of inadequate care prior to adoption are yet unknown. Some of these children will most likely display medical conditions or developmental delays requiring intervention before or after school entry.

Price (2000), for example, found the average time at home before developmental or physical issues became apparent was 2.62 and 2.64 years, respectively for her sample of 798 children from Russia and other eastern European countries. The mean time at home for emotional issues to surface, however, was 3.67 years. Moreover, continuing delays in motor, cognitive, language, and socioemotional skills have been identified by researchers in numerous studies of children adopted from Russia, the former Soviet states, and China (Albers et al., 1997; Clauss & Baxter, 1997; Groze & Ileana, 1996; Miller & Hendrie, 2000; Morison et al., 1995; Rojewski & Rojewski, 2001; Rutter, 1998). Length of institutionalization prior to adoption was related to developmental delays in most of these studies.

Some children are currently receiving special services for their health and developmental needs. Groze and Ileana (1996) found that 81 of the 122 Romanian school-age children in their sample were in special education classes, with 69 children having learning disabilities. Clauss and Baxter (1997), too, found that 10% of the 206 families returning their survey indicated their child had some type of learning problem in school. Johnson and his colleagues warned that early intervention and special programs may help children maximize their potential, but the extent to which children can recover from these delays is not known (Albers et al., 1997).

To minimize the effects of institutional delays, Lemer (2001) suggested that parents seek primary and secondary therapies according to the unique needs of the child and the family budget. For example, for children ages 0 to 3, she recommended nutritional supplementation under the care of a physician and sensory integration training with an occupational therapist as primary interventions. Speech and language therapy was her suggested secondary level of intervention. For children ages 4 to 7, Lemer recommended both sensory integration training and speech language therapy as primary interventions.

As children age, 8- to 12-year-olds might receive academic assistance as the primary intervention, with continued speech/language therapy and psychological services as needed. For children over the age of 12, academic assistance and help with socioemotional skills become key forms of intervention.

Children of intercountry adoptions may display delays in language, motor, social, and cognitive skills that are understood by teachers when they become familiar with the background of the child. Many of these children catch up as rapidly as they can with *appropriately challenging* expectations and levels of assistance from their parents and teachers. However, *parents and teachers must remember that these children may be chronologically older than their developmental level*, thus expectations must be adjusted accordingly. Less easily understood and more unsettling, however, may be the unusual behaviors exhibited by some children such as stealing or hoarding food or possessions, aggressiveness, and sensory or tactile defensiveness. Lack of socioemotional readiness may ultimately affect the child's school success more than any other factor.

CONCLUSION

Children of intercountry adoptions, particularly those from institutional environments, are at risk for successful school performance. Many of these children experience physical conditions related to inadequate nutrition and medical care or to maternal alcohol abuse and/or environmental toxins. Delays in motor, cognitive, language, and socioemotional skills related to institutional living are common months and years after arrival home. Sensory integrative and attachment disorders, although uncommon, are observed among children arriving from Romania, Russia, and eastern European countries. The long-term effects of these delays and the ameliorative effects of the adoptive family are only now beginning to be explored. Many children will do well; however, early intervention during the preschool years and special assistance as the child advances through school may be necessary to optimize outcomes for others.

Chapter 3

Adoption and Institutionalization Issues in the School Years

According to experts, children adopted internationally must be considered "special needs," at least temporarily (Babb & Laws, 1997; Bascom & McKelvey, 1997; Groze & Ileana, 1996). Those coming from institutionalized environments are particularly at risk, especially those adopted beyond the age of 2. Approximately 25% of these children will have no difficulties beyond those to be expected as they adapt to a new language and culture (Federici, 2000). For many, however, some difficulties will be immediately apparent, and for others, problems may show up after they have been in their homes for months or even years. Still other unknown difficulties may not arise until these children go up the grades in school and are compared by teachers to other children of the same age. Children of intercountry adoptions may, for example, experience the following delays placing them at risk in school:

- Gross and fine motor skill or sensory integration delays make these children appear clumsy and awkward and make age-appropriate coloring, cutting, and neat handwriting difficult.
- Language delays for some children are the result of little stimulation in an orphanage environment. Other children are simply learning English and

cannot understand the teacher's directions or the language of classroom instruction to the same extent as other children. These misunderstandings can lead to frustration, failure, behavior problems, or inappropriate placement in a special education program. An apparent fluency in speaking English can also easily deceive adults into believing that these children know and understand more than they really do.

- Cognitive delays can affect these children's ability to think, plan, and problem-solve. Cognitive delays impact their ability to grasp new concepts and vocabulary and adversely affect all areas of learning in school.
- Socioemotional delays make these children appear less mature than their same-age peers. Children with socioemotional deficits may not fit in. They may be aggressive or shy and withdrawn, or they may lack social skills and have poor interpersonal relationships with peers and teachers.

Despite these difficulties noted in many children adopted internationally, the long-term effects of their preadoptive living environments on school performance is yet unknown. *Parents and teachers must not automatically assume that just because children come from an adoption abroad that they will have difficulty with learning and behavior in school.* The long-term healing effects of children's personalities and of their new families, for example, are only now being explored. Some children simply have "easy" temperaments (Thomas & Chess, 1984). That is, they possess inborn, genetic personality factors giving them the strength and ability to adapt to the environment. Children born with easier temperamental characteristics are more able to overcome adversity and "bounce back" than are those with more "difficult" temperaments. Moreover, the impact of early adversity may be lessened to some degree by the presence of an attentive, supportive, consistent caregiver (Luthar & Zigler, 1991; Werner & Smith, 1989, 1992) and a cohesive nurturing family (McGuinness, 2000). Thus, children with "easy" temperaments may be more likely to elicit positive attention from caregivers than are children with "difficult" personalities, improving their resiliency or their ability to rebound from early harsh surroundings once they are settled into their new homes.

Clearly, it is not yet known how children of intercountry adoption will fare in school, but it is clear that adoption will affect these children throughout their lifetime. Children adopted in the United States often experience grief, a sense of loss, and sometimes anger and confusion as they come to grips with what adoption means and begin to search for their identity and a "sense of self" (Brodzinsky, 1990;

Brodzinsky, Schechter, & Henig, 1992; Melina, 1998). Although most of what is known about the effects of adoption on children comes from studies of American children and not children who are adopted internationally, children of intercountry adoption will likely experience each of these sources of stress as well. For them, however, developmental delays, early deprivation, and language and cultural differences may compound the "normal" adoption issues experienced by American children. Still other children may experience ambivalence regarding their birth country or mixed feelings about their racial identity if their parents are of a different race (e.g., the child is Asian and the parents are Caucasian). Parents and teachers must also remember that adoption and institutionalization issues such as these may surface repeatedly and interact with one another, affecting children throughout their school years.

Having parents and teachers who understand how adoption issues such as those described in Table 3.1 may reappear during the school years is of tremendous importance for the success of these children. Parents and teachers must recognize, however, that *difficulties experienced by children who are adopted are often simply developmental issues, and not the result of adoption itself* (Schaffer & Lindstrom, 1989). The 2-year-old will have temper tantrums, the 4- or 5-year-old girl will argue with her mother over wearing a dress versus pants, and the adolescent will disagree with parents as he or she establishes an identity. These behaviors are typical of all children and should not be viewed as the result of adoption, or even international adoption, alone! Nevertheless, parents and school personnel who understand that the effects of intercountry adoption may complicate other adoption issues are better prepared to help youngsters deal with any difficulties if they do arise at school.

❊ THE PRESCHOOL YEARS

Attachment, separation, and the development of language are crucial tasks for every infant and toddler. Children adopted from abroad as infants will no doubt have the same developmental tasks. The infant and toddler need to develop trust in the caregiver and need to know that their world is a safe, secure place. They also begin the process of separation by testing limits when parents say "no," by having temper tantrums, and by protesting when parents must leave them to go elsewhere. These are normal behaviors for any child from birth through age 2.

Table 3.1
Developmental Issues Associated with Adoption

Age in Years	Major Developmental Issues
Birth to 3	Lacks comprehension of reproduction and adoption. Loves to hear his or her adoption story. May retell the adoption story to anyone who will listen. Feels he or she is "special."
4 to 6	Knows babies come from their mothers. Has a beginning understanding that mother did not give birth to him or her. Is beginning to understand that most peers are not adopted. Notices differences in skin color and other major physical characteristics.
7 to 11	Understands that adoption means relinquishment by the birth mother. May experience a sense of loss or grief for birth parents. Wants to feel same as peers, but may feel different. May be teased. Questions parents about his or her adoption.
12 and older	Understands reproduction and the many reasons why birth parents may relinquish children. May either actively resist or "over-identify" with national or cultural origins. Seeks his or her identity. Wonders about his or her biological roots.

Children who are adopted beyond age 2 may also exhibit the same types of behaviors as they begin the process of attachment and separation. For children of intercountry adoption, these processes may be complicated by an inability to understand the language, the effects of inconsistent caregiving in an institutional environment, or cultural differences in how infants are treated. Additionally, children as young as infancy experience the effects of loss and grief, becoming apathetic and less responsive when they are removed from the familiar sights, sounds, and smells of their surroundings. Regardless of how impoverished that setting may have been, it was of course still "home" to the child. These children may also have passed through many time zones traveling to their new homes and will need time to adjust to new sleeping and eating patterns as well (Gilman, 1992).

Typical children between the ages of 3 and 5 continue their separation from parents and begin to examine their world in earnest. They can also be quite stubborn and aggressive with one another as they learn to share and play together. As they go to day care and preschool, they make new friends outside of the family and they may become fearful of being lost or abandoned by their parents or captured by the monster under the bed! Children adopted from abroad during the preschool years often may be even more fearful (and occasionally far less fearful to the concern of parents!) than other same-age children, lacking the secure base, concepts, and language to safely negotiate new environments. These children benefit from routine and structure at home with their parents for several months before they are introduced to many new people and to the demands of a new setting such as a day-care center or preschool.

Preschool-aged children of intercountry adoption may even actively resist settings containing many other children, including day-care centers, preschool, and bible school, for a period of time after arrival home. Perhaps they fear separation and abandonment—that they will be left with the other children as before. This fear is certainly understandable when one considers that most preschool and kindergarten teachers request parents provide an extra set of clothing in case of "accidents" and a floor mat or cot for daily naps! Or, perhaps the children are simply overstimulated, confused, or unable to understand the language and activities of the other children. Moreover, some children adopted at this age may grieve for playmates from the orphanage and therefore resist friendships with other children. Children in institutional care can certainly bond to one another as closely as if they were brother and sister. Laura (see Chapter 1) and another little girl, for example, grieved for one another after Laura's departure from their orphanage in Russia, and both were delighted when they were reunited 4 years later in the United States!

Indeed, children of intercountry adoptions can experience extremely traumatic events and profound losses at an early age causing them to grieve or to have night terrors for a very long time. Only after they develop trust in their parents and enough language to communicate can they begin to disclose their stories more fully. French (1986), for example, related the story of loss slowly exposed during rides to nursery school by her daughter, Maria, adopted at age 4 from

Bangladesh. She recounted that her daughter asked questions such as "What happen when you die?" or made statements like "I used to knock on door and ask for rice" before showing her mother a picture of someone apparently shot and asking "Mommy, what this mean?" When her mother replied, "Well it looks like someone was shot with a gun, then fell down and died," Maria replied, "Yes, that how my mommy died" (p. 273). Later, she remembered that she had an older sister, although she did not remember until several weeks later her sister's name or the circumstances that led to her being removed from her sister on the streets where they were living and to her placement in an orphanage.

Most experts agree that preschoolers do not really understand their adoption (Brodzinsky, Singer, & Braff, 1984). They are frequently curious and ask questions about where babies come from, but they do not yet have the cognitive abilities or maturity to understand reproduction and the many reasons why a birth mother might choose to place her child for adoption. Parents also disagree as to whether or not to tell their preschooler about his or her adoption; however, experts recommend that parents answer a child's questions as honestly as possible, within the limits of the child's understanding and without "over explaining," as questions arise (Gilman, 1992; Melina, 1998; Schaffer & Lindstrom, 1989). As a matter of fact, parents report that the frequency with which they discuss adoption increases with their child's age (Rojewski & Rojewski, 2001).

Most children of intercountry adoptions placed with their parents between the ages of 3 and 5 will need to know a "simple" version of their adoption story immediately. This can be accomplished with simple words and pictures or through a translator in the birth country. Quite often, the story becomes a favorite bedtime tale for the preschooler: "Once upon a time, there was a little girl named Sveta. When Sveta was born, her birth mother couldn't take care of any baby at all, so she placed Sveta in a children's home in Russia with many other little boys and girls. *And,* once upon a time a mom and a dad in America were sad because they wanted a little girl to be their daughter. One day the mom and dad saw a picture of little Sveta. They wanted Sveta to be their own little daughter to love forever and ever. So they flew all the way to Russia on an airplane, and they traveled for many miles on a train, and they adopted Sveta. Then, Sveta went all the way back on the train and the airplane to her new home with her mom and dad who loved her and took care of her forever!"

In order to prevent young children who are adopted from falsely concluding that some children are adopted and some children are born, parents must explain as simply as possible in the adoption story that the child was born first and then adopted. Additionally, children of intercountry adoption can sometimes erroneously conclude that they arrived in their family "by airplane" or that "some nannies gave me to my mother and father in the airport (or at the hotel)." For other children raised in an institutional setting, the concept of "family" is lacking because these children had many different "mamas" or "nannies" and may have seen relatively few men. Thus, parents and preschool teachers may need time to help the child gain an understanding of "mother," "father," "parents," and "families" before the adoption story can be completely understood. Obviously, adoption stories must be carefully considered in advance to include the child's birth and placement in the new family, both in terms the child can understand.

Brodzinsky and his colleagues (Brodzinsky, Singer, & Braff, 1984; Brodzinsky et al., 1992) cautioned that children of this age may simply parrot their adoption story with very little understanding. As a matter of fact, children of this age have been known to tell their adoption tale to anyone who will listen! Children of this age enjoy feeling special and may gleefully show off prized possessions brought from their birth countries. As children of intercountry adoption tell their "special" adoption stories to others in the day-care or preschool setting, however, other children may become confused and ask questions like "Where is your *real* mommy?" Although very young children will not be upset by these questions, children of kindergarten age may begin to experience some anxiety over their "different" status (Brodzinsky, 1990).

Too, children as young as 3 or 4 do indeed notice differences between themselves and others, with skin color often one of the first physical features to be noticed (Melina, 1998). Children from Guatemala, India, or Asian countries having caucasian parents may be asked by peers, for example, why they don't look like their mommy or daddy. Similarly, little girls from orphanages, particularly those in Russia and the former Soviet states, often have such shortly cropped hair that other children might ask why they look like boys or why "that boy" is wearing girls' clothing. My daughter, for example, wore a string of beads over her head and hanging down her back for several months after arriving home at age 4½, refusing to take them off. We finally realized that the beads were her "hair," helping her to look like the other little girls with long hair she saw all around her!

All preschool-age children who are adopted, then, must cope with grief and loss and accomplish many important tasks. These include attachment, separation, a rudimentary recognition of individual differences, and assimilation of the adoption story. Parents and preschool teachers must be sensitive to the additional and unique needs of children who are adopted from abroad including language learning, cultural differences, and the effects of institutionalized living. Young children from institutions may, for example, cling to one parent and reject the other or evidence an overwhelming need to keep parents within their sight as they learn to establish relationships (Bascom & McKelvey, 1997). Yet, preschoolers of intercountry adoption are first and foremost children; therefore, their parents and teachers must understand that not all behaviors they exhibit are necessarily related to their adoption.

�֍ THE ELEMENTARY SCHOOL YEARS

As children move from kindergarten at age 5 to the elementary grades from ages 6 through 10 or 11, they become increasingly separated from their families and more involved in events at school or activities with friends. They also become able to think in increasingly complex ways. Developing academic and sports skills, competition, comparisons to others, and learning to form satisfying friendships are all hallmarks of child development during the elementary school years (Greenspan, 1993).

According to Greenspan (1993), as children become more attuned to others and to activities outside the home, they begin to weigh their status within the peer group. That is, they begin to gauge their own self-worth and self-esteem from how they compare to their peers at school and at play. Being the same as one's peers is important to this age group. Competition to be the "first" or the "best" and teasing also frequently become ways of establishing status among peers.

As children who are adopted begin to compare themselves to their peers, they begin to realize that most children are not adopted, and that this fact makes them different. Unfortunately, this feeling of difference comes at a time when children interpret being "different" as being "not quite as good as" their friends. Being different can make children at this age the recipient of teasing. At the same time, their ability to think more abstractly leads them to the realization that adoption and birth are two alternative ways to join a family and to the understanding that placement in their family also meant relinquishment by someone else (Brodzinsky, 1990; Brodzinsky et al., 1992). The realization that something must have gone so wrong that their birth mother could not raise them precipitates an increasing sense of loss and grief. Between the ages of 7 and 11, children begin to see the biological nature and continuity of families. Children of this age wrestle with questions, whether or not they are voiced, having to do with a loss of relationships and biological connections. They might ask, for example, "Why didn't my birth mother keep me?" Often, children will assume the blame themselves, incorrectly thinking that they must have been "bad" or that something was "wrong" with them for this to have happened. Children in this age group wonder "Why me?" "What really happened?" "What is my birth mother like?" "What is my birth father like?" "Who else is in my birth family?" (Dellisanti, 1994). These children may also worry about the permanence of their adoption, how to handle teasing from peers, and whether adoption is or is not as "good" as being born into a family.

As children struggle with emotions of loss and grief for what might have been, they may be inattentive to parents or teachers. They may "tune in and out" at school, or they may even resist certain topics like subtraction because the term *take away* conjures up unpleasant memories or fears (Maskew, 1999). They may also experience separation anxiety, running fearfully through the house, for example, to find their parents when they are unexpectedly out of sight.

In addition, they may fantasize about their birth mothers or fathers. They might, for example, react to being told by their mother that they cannot have a particular pair of expensive shoes by yelling, "I'm going to go find my birth mother. She would be nicer than you and get me those shoes!" Inside, however, these children might also be worrying about abandonment by their parents or the loss of their love. The self-esteem of these children is often on the line as they experience mixed feelings of guilt, grief, love, loss, and shame. The once prized and publicly shared adoption story now may become a source of embarrassment and these children may prefer that their adoption be kept a secret from others, especially peers.

Children of intercountry adoptions, like their counterparts adopted here in the United States, may handle these mixed emotions and questions in different ways, enjoying attending events with other children who are adopted, preferring to keep their worries to themselves, or openly challenging their parents or teachers. Children from an intercountry adoption, however, may have additional sources of stress and loss during these important school years. For example, some children may wonder or fantasize about the birth country and experience sadness over losing connections with that country and its culture (Register, 1991; Trolley, 1995). As with the preschooler, children adopted at the age of 4, 5, or beyond experience the loss of familiar sights, sounds, smells, and people. Moreover, most parents adopting children internationally do not speak the child's language; therefore, the children also lose their birth country language and patterns of thought and behavior (Hough, 2000). Even the familiar comfort of the original name might be lost as many children are given new Americanized names after adoption.

Additionally, children of intercountry adoption may experience conflicting emotions regarding their adoption and their racial and ethnic identity (Melina, 1998). Children adopted from India, Korea, Guatemala, or China by caucasian parents, for example, simply cannot keep their adoption a secret—it is immediately apparent to all who meet their family (Brodzinsky et al., 1992). According to Register (1991), children adopted transculturally and transracially will be *hyphenated* children (e.g., Asian-American)—children who feel bonds to both cultures but who may often feel torn between the two. These children may be proud of their Chinese or Vietnamese heritage, for example, but nevertheless find it difficult to reconcile their pride with a desire not to stand out as different from their peers. Moreover, these children may experience subtle racial stereotyping—expectations by teachers, for example, that they will be model students in school or excel at math simply because they are Chinese or Korean.

Children adopted at the age of 4 or 5 or beyond may also experience a sense of culture shock and a feeling of loss of control. They had no say, for example, in being transported from a familiar environment to a new country. Children coming from developing countries may find their beautiful home and room full of toys, busy highways, blaring televisions and radios, or well-stocked shelves in stores to be confusing, overstimulating, distracting, or sources of anxiety and guilt as they remember the living conditions of those they left behind. They may find it difficult to make choices and decisions, to engage in play, or to be spontaneous when they have never been permitted to make choices, to decide something for themselves, to play, or to be spontaneous before. Too, children coming from institutionalized environments may be initially fearful of many things

American children take for granted including seat belts, getting dirty, pets, and sleeping alone. Automobiles, trees, rain, playground equipment, and even bathtubs can all provoke fear in children who have rarely or never been outside their room in an orphanage. Moreover, some children fear that they will not have enough to eat, resulting in stealing, hoarding, or hiding food or gorging themselves for a period of time after they arrive home. Behaviors such as these, tantrums, or withdrawal can signal culture shock in elementary-age children, but can also easily be misinterpreted by parents or teachers as "misbehavior."

Additionally, children with less developed motor, social, and language skills are at a disadvantage when competing with peers. They may be teased, for example, when they say "Good morling" instead of "Good morning" or when they do not know their letters, numbers, or concepts other children knew as preschoolers. Six-, 7-, or 8-year-olds who are catching up may still be socially and cognitively more like younger children and prefer watching *Barney* or *Blues Clues* on television or playing with blocks as they adjust to an unfamiliar world. Such teasing and daily "failure" compared to peers can result in frustration and a low self-esteem, particularly for children who may already have a fragile self-esteem following years of seeing other younger children leave the orphanage with their parents.

So, too, can the process of learning a new language. As children lose their first language and replace it with English, they may speak their new language quite fluently. Parents and teachers may overlook more serious language delays, attributing any difficulty simply to the process of learning English (Gindis, 2000; Hough, 2000). In addition, parents and teachers may hear how well the child speaks English and fail to realize that conversational language develops faster than the complex, abstract language of instruction. Consequently, these children miss out on much information exchanged through social and instructional interactions in the classroom and they may fall even further behind their classmates academically (see Chapter 5). The second or third grader, for example, may cry at home asking, "How come everybody else knows that?" or "How come everyone else 'gets it' and I don't?" Saying "Everyone else in the class has had 7 (or 8 or 9) years of speaking English and learning what American children know and you've only had 3 (or 4, etc.)" can help, but that information can't lessen the pain of not measuring up to one's more advanced peers.

Children of intercountry adoption can and do make friends, however. McGuinness (2000) examined the relationship between low birth weight and institutional living and the later social and school competence of children ages 6 to 9 adopted from the former Soviet Union. She found, for example, that most of the children in her sample of 105 scored well on a test of social competence, although 35% of the children had lower than average scores compared to never institutionalized children. On this test, parents were asked to rate their child's behavior in areas such as "has a group of friends" or "has a best friend of the same sex." Just over 57% of the children in her sample also were attending some form of special class (e.g., speech/language therapy) in addition to their regular class at school. Mc-Guinness stated that parents and families certainly provide an enriched environment, lessen the impact of risk factors, and improve the child's competence. Nevertheless, children having lengthy stays in institutionalized environments, poor pre- and postnatal health care, low birth weight, a history of maternal alcohol abuse, exposure to environmental toxins, or language delays may be at risk for making friends and adjusting well at school. They may also be at increased risk for learning disabilities or attention deficit hyperactivity disorder (ADHD) during the elementary school years (Groze & Ileana, 1996).

Learning Disabilities

Children with learning disabilities have average or even above average intellectual ability; however, they have a great deal of difficulty learning in one or more specific academic areas in school given the typical means of instruction. Students with learning disabilities, for example, might be quite good at mathematics, but unable to read despite ample opportunity and sound instruction. Or, they might have handwriting that is highly unreadable, making it difficult for them to produce legible work, to align numbers in order to add or subtract, or to take understandable notes in class. Moreover, many students with learning disabilities have trouble planning, organizing, and monitoring their own behavior. Thus, they might have trouble studying spelling words or organizing and memorizing information for a test without someone teaching them a specific strategy for doing so. The identifying criteria for a learning disability most often used by the schools is an uneven pattern of development—a significant discrepancy between the child's intellectual ability and his or her performance in one or more specific academic areas.

The "best" definition of learning disabilities is much debated. The definition used most often, however, is that contained in The Individuals with Disabilities Education Act (IDEA, 1997), the federal law mandating special education programs for children with disabilities in the public schools. IDEA defines a "specific learning disability" as follows:

> a disorder in one or more of the basic psychological processes involved in understanding or in using language, spoken or written, which disorder may manifest itself in an imperfect ability to listen, think, speak, read, write, spell, or do mathematical calculations. Such term includes such conditions as perceptual disabilities, brain injury, minimal brain dysfunction, dyslexia, and developmental aphasia. Such term does not include a learning problem that is primarily the result of visual, hearing, or motor disabilities, of mental retardation, of emotional disturbance, or of environmental, cultural, or economic disadvantage. (SEC.602.26)

Thus, a learning disability may not be solely the result of low cognitive ability, of an emotional problem, or of poor instruction or a deprived environment. Nor can the problem be due to difficulty seeing, hearing, or moving. The implication is that despite good intelligence, hearing, and vision, these children have difficulty processing (or interpreting and making sense of) and remembering the information they hear or see due to some unknown neurological difficulty. Thus, children with excellent hearing but who have learning disabilities might have trouble detecting the difference between two similar-sounding words such as "think" and "thing." Similarly, they might have trouble remembering oral directions involving multiple steps such as "Please get your reading book from the shelf, take it to your table, and open it to page 45." Too, children with learning disabilities have normal vision but might be unable to recognize letters or simple words after much practice or have difficulty integrating their visual and motor processes to copy a letter or a number legibly. Sometimes, parents and teachers will see terms applied to children with learning disabilities to describe their particular learning problems in school such as *dyslexia* (i.e., a severe reading difficulty), *dyscalculia* (i.e., a severe problem with mathematics), or *dysgraphia* (i.e., illegible handwriting).

Approximately 5% of the school-aged population has some form of learning disability. The majority of children with learning disabilities has difficulty with reading. As specified in the IDEA (1997) definition, an inability to use language, spoken or written, is an underlying problem for most children with learning disabilities. Unfortunately, difficulty understanding spoken language or problems learning to read and write affect all other areas of academic learning, including mathematics, and make school performance increasingly more difficult and frustrating as these children advance in school. As a matter of fact, children with learning disabilities are at risk compared to their peers for dropping out of school, and later, for reduced wages on the job (Blackorby & Wagner, 1996).

Obviously, for children who are just learning to speak English, the diagnosis of a learning disability cannot be determined solely on their inability to understand and use spoken language! IDEA (1997) prohibits children from being placed in special education for limited English proficiency alone (see Chapter 5). Moreover, parents and school professionals must remember that sometimes children who are adopted are simply thinking about what adoption means; thus, they may have difficulty paying attention and learning at that particular time. Nonetheless, if children with learning disabilities do have some sort of neurological difficulty (e.g., a difference in metabolic activity in the brain) underlying their trouble learning in school, one might expect that children from intercountry adoptions might be at increased risk. Furthermore, approximately 20% to 30% of children with learning disabilities also have an ADHD affecting their ability to learn and behave at school (Riccio, Gonzalez, & Hynd, 1994).

ADHD

Children with ADHD may be hyperactive, impulsive, or have a difficult time delaying their responses (Barkley, 1993). They may act before considering the consequences of their actions, become easily distracted by others or by their own thoughts, or cause constant disruption. According to the American Psychiatric Association (APA, 1994), for a child to be considered as having ADHD his or her behaviors must be more severe and frequent than that of other children at the same developmental level. Additionally, the child's behaviors must have occurred across many different settings before the age of 7 and persisted for at least 6 months. Furthermore, the APA (1994) specifies two different types of ADHDs:

1. The Predominantly Inattentive Type—The child doesn't appear to listen, makes careless mistakes, is easily distracted, can't sustain at-

tention for an age-appropriate period of time, or has difficulty organizing and carrying out activities.

2. The Predominantly Hyperactive-Impulsive Type—The child is constantly in motion, fidgeting, running, interrupting others, and unable to wait his or her turn.

Most children with ADHD are of the combined type, exhibiting at least six of the behavioral characteristics listed by the APA for both the Inattentive and Hyperactive-Impulsive types of disorders. In addition, ADHD is considered a lifelong disorder, affecting the child's success in school, in relationships, in the community, and on the job (Lerner, Lowenthal, & Lerner, 1995).

At school, for example, children with ADHD frequently demonstrate delayed gross motor coordination, problems with frustration tolerance, and difficulty regulating their emotions (Barkley, 1998). They often engage in disruptive behaviors in the classroom, have trouble achieving academically, and repeat one or more grades in school. Children with ADHD tend not to persist on tasks, particularly when the task produces frustration, and 30% to 40% of these students are placed in special education programs for various disabilities often associated with ADHD. That is, during the school years, ADHD frequently occurs along with other disabilities such as learning disabilities and emotional/behavioral disorders (McKinney, Montague, & Hocutt, 1993; Reid, Maag, Vasa, & Wright, 1994; Shaywitz & Shaywitz, 1988). Additionally, the APA (1994) estimates that 3% to 5% of the school-aged population may have ADHD hindering their ability to progress through school and to graduate.

Although the cause of ADHD is unknown, most experts now agree that it is probably biological, neurochemical, or genetic in nature. Barkley (1998), for example, noted that ADHD tends to run in families. Moreover, some children with ADHD have a deficiency in the production of neurotransmitters such as norepinephrine or dopamine necessary for regulating attention (Hynd, Hern, Voeller, & Marshall, 1991). A reduced blood flow to an area of the brain regulating motor activity (Teicher et al., 2000) and a deficiency in metabolizing substances such as glucose in the brain (Zametkin et al., 1990) are two additional causes of ADHD currently under investigation. As a matter of fact, Castellanos (1999) characterized ADHD as a deficiency in self-regulation resulting from genetic factors, the maturation of the brain, and dysfunctional neurotransmitter systems.

Children of intercountry adoption may be at greater risk for

ADHD than their same-aged peers given the risk factors frequently seen in these youngsters such as low birth weight, exposure to environmental toxins like lead, or the poor pre- and postnatal health care many received prior to adoption. Additionally, ADHD in the birth mother may have led to an inability to survive and parent effectively in a depressed economy or to a "diagnosis" resulting in institutionalization for her child. Obviously, however, any child may exhibit the behaviors associated with ADHD as he or she adjusts to a new family and new surroundings during the months following adoption. Difficulty paying attention and activity levels over or under what is "typical" of children at a particular developmental level are frequently observed in children from institutional backgrounds after arrival home. Moreover, any child may have difficulty paying attention as he or she thinks about adoption. Therefore, parents and school personnel must not automatically assume that inattentive or restless children of intercountry adoption have ADHD. This is a determination that can be made only by the physician and only after a period of adjustment and careful observation.

Regardless of the cause, however, children with ADHD are likely to experience difficulty in school, at home, and in the community. Unfortunately, ADHD may also make the period of adjustment more difficult for the child and family and compound the effects of institutionalization, making these children less able to adapt, overcome early deprivation, and thrive in their new families and schools, particularly as they approach adolescence.

❋ THE SECONDARY SCHOOL YEARS

As children enter middle or junior high school and high school, they continue to separate from their families. Establishing a solid sense of autonomy and identity is the major developmental task of adolescence. Children from ages 11 or 12 and up must become comfortable in their ability to stand on their own, and they may vacillate between wanting to be an adult and wanting to remain a child. They are defining their position in the family, in the community, and in society.

Adolescents typically "try on" many different beliefs, activities, and styles of living, and they frequently question the values and habits of their parents and teachers. Girls, for example, may prefer to dye their hair blue, get a body tattoo, or pierce their nose and tongue if these styles are not representative of their parents' generation. Similarly, boys might shave their heads or wear an earring. Adolescents also form tight social circles at school that encourage similar styles of dress and behavior and that are often intolerant of anyone who is perceived as different.

If adolescence is ordinarily a period of questioning one's identity, relationships, and physical appearance, it is a time of particular vulnerability for adolescents who have been adopted. Teenagers who are adopted and forming relationships with the opposite sex are facing biological questions such as "Who do I really look like?" and "Are there genetic tendencies I have inherited that I don't know about that might affect my life or my children?" (Dellisanti, 1994). Adolescents who are adopted wonder "Where did I get my talent in music (or painting)?" or "Why do I freckle so easily?" when these are not talents or traits evident in their family (Melina, 1998). Teenagers who are adopted cannot take comfort in knowing that they are "just like Aunt Sue or Grandpa Ben," and in fact, they might believe acceptance of such comments to be downright hypocritical!

In addition, as adolescents separate from their family, they might question family loyalties and values. As teenagers question or even openly rebel, they are also asking, "Can I still be a part of my family?" and "Can I be a part of my biological family and still have my family?" Sometimes adolescents who are adopted find their parents to be easy targets, blaming them for their confusion with statements like "I didn't ask to move here with you" (Melina, 1998). Many are angry at their birth mothers, viewing their placement for adoption as rejection rather than as a demonstration of love. Some decide to begin a search for their biological roots at this time and others do not. According to Melina (1998), in most instances, adolescents simply want information to help them develop a sense of self, and not an actual meeting with members of the birth family.

Intercountry adoption may complicate normal adolescent adoption issues for children adopted at any age. For example, they may bring with them "survival" behaviors learned after many years of taking care of themselves and competing for attention or food in an orphanage or on the streets, causing them to behave in an independent manner resistant to adult directions or to concerned parenting. Similarly, children of intercountry adoption who come to the United States as preteens or adolescents are likely to experience culture shock much like the elementary-aged child. They may experience confusion or anxiety in unfamiliar situations or even feelings of guilt over their new abundance. Conversely, they may have an inflated image of the

United States and what their life "should" be like, becoming disappointed or rebellious when they don't have the DVD player, computer, cell phone, and other amenities they imagined themselves having (Maskew, 1999). They are also likely to bring with them cultural characteristics that may clash with patterns of behavior in their new family and school such as the following:

- The appropriate role for males and females or beliefs about touching, hugging, kissing, or sleeping (e.g., sleeping on the floor or an inability to sleep without others in the room)
- Prohibitions about discussing unpleasant experiences or negative emotions that can be misperceived as insolence or apathy
- An attitude that time and punctuality are relatively unimportant, which can be misconstrued as "laziness" or "disrespect"
- Eating habits (i.e., eating on the floor, or with the hands, or gulping food quickly; food preferences at odds with what peers typically bring to school in their lunch boxes; discomfort with table conversation or dining with adults).

For children of intercountry adoption who entered their homes at a younger age, the normal search for an identity separate from their parents may lead them to "overidentify" with their birth country as they become adolescents (Deacon, 1997). They may, for example, prefer to dress, eat, and assume the traditions of their birthplace. As a matter of fact, many parents of children adopted internationally say it is important for their children to identify with both the American and birth country cultures (Maskew, 1999; Rojewski & Rojewski, 2001; Trolley, Wallin, & Hansen, 1995). Thus, they try to promote this connection through providing artifacts or reading materials from the birth country, celebrating holidays with traditional foods or activities, taking classes to learn their child's language, or attending cultural events or culture camps. On the other hand, some children may actively reject their birth countries and cultures completely in an attempt to establish values and habits different than parents or in order to be perceived the same as peers. These youngsters now may actively resist their parents' efforts to go to cultural events or ethnic restaurants.

Unfortunately, children of intercountry adoption sometimes experience outright racial or ethnic prejudice in the form of comments directed toward them, to their parents, or to their country of birth (Rojewski & Rojewski, 2001). When they are young, these comments may go unnoticed; however, insensitive comments and questions may be particularly hurtful to adolescents, coming at a time when they are searching for their identity. According to Wardle (1990), "While the white American parent and her foreign adopted child see their differences as national and cultural, much of society responds to the difference of physical characteristics, especially skin color" (p. 45). Racial and ethnic stereotyping and bigotry may be more evident when children are adopted transracially as well as transculturally, but comments regarding adopting "communists" have still been leveled at parents of children from Russia and other eastern European countries, even when their children look like their biological offspring. Additionally, adolescents may experience mixed feelings of guilt, grief, or shame regarding their ethnic origins when they read articles or hear television accounts of poverty, war, natural disasters, or illegal activities in their birth country (Pertman, 2000; Schaffer & Lindstrom, 1989).

Some authorities raise ethical questions—concern, for example, that children of intercountry adoptions may have difficulty with self-esteem, friendships, and racial or ethnic identity when they are adolescents unless their right to their ethnic and racial identity is preserved (Babb, 1999; Westhues & Cohen, 1998). Nevertheless, Cohen and Westhues (1995) reported that children adopted by caucasian parents in Canada from countries such as Korea and Bangladesh were no different than their Canadian born siblings in self-esteem, friendships, or success in school. Similarly, Altstein and his colleagues (1994) found adolescents adopted primarily from Korea had mostly caucasian friends and a sense that all adolescents struggle with who they are regardless of their ethnicity or adoption.

Unknown to date, of course, is how the newly adopted children like Jennifer, Laura, and Olivia from institutions in Russia, Romania, other eastern European countries, and China will fare as they become adolescents and grapple with their biological roots, their previous institutionalization, and their ethnic and cultural heritage. Most likely, some of these children will be proud of their roots and others will be "Americanized" and prefer it that way. Moreover, these children as adolescents will find any search for their biological roots to be difficult if not impossible. In countries such as Russia, for example, adoptions are still "closed" despite the information their parents may have about their birth, and political conditions and anti-American sentiments may produce barriers to searching. For many of these children, however, abandonment to an institution means little, if any, information will be available regarding their birth parents, birth date, actual birth place, or the context of their birth. These children must live with many unknowns, without a baby picture, a picture of their birth mother, the name of the town or hospital where they were born, or an exact birth date. At best, some of these children will return to visit their birth country, birth town, or orphanage and some will continue to maintain connections with other children from their group in the same orphanage. As these children attain adolescence and adulthood, some may experience a profound sense of loss and incompleteness as they attempt to reconcile their unknown past with the positive future offered by their families through their adoption (Trolley, 1995).

CONCLUSION

Children adopted at any age throughout the United States are likely to experience recurring issues associated with their adoption as they grow older. Grief, loss, and feelings of an "unknown identity" are common to individuals who are adopted. As children think about these difficult issues and make comparisons between themselves and others at school, they may be lost in thought and find it difficult to pay attention and learn. Children of intercountry adoptions likely experience the same emotions of grief, loss, and confusion regarding their identity, and they may also expend mental energy during the school hours thinking about their adoption. These children, however, are likely to have come from institutionalized backgrounds and to have less information about their birth families than children adopted within the United States, complicating their search for answers to their questions as they grapple with these difficult emotions and adoption-related issues. Moreover, children from neglectful backgrounds may have developmental delays, early deprivation, poor pre- and postnatal health care, exposure to toxins, and language and cultural differences that may compound the "normal" adoption issues experienced by American children.

Parents and school personnel must recognize, however, that difficulties experienced by most children who are adopted, whether in the United States or internationally, are often simply developmental issues, and not the result of adoption itself. Other difficulties in school may be related to the children's inner thoughts regarding adoption, but not to their status as children of intercountry adoptions. Although parents and teachers must be sensitive to the additional, unique needs of children who are adopted from abroad, particularly language learning, the effects of institutionalized living, and cultural differences, they should ask the following questions if problems arise rather than jumping to hasty conclusions:

1. Is the problem this child is having simply a "normal" behavior typical of all children at that developmental level (e.g., kindergarten boys are "wiggly" and adolescents "try on" different values)?

2. Is the problem this child is having related to "normal" adoption issues (e.g., the child is inattentive or irritable because he or she is thinking about the birth family or birth country)?

3. Could this problem be related to differences of language or culture (e.g., the older Korean boy who "bosses" his younger siblings or the child who is frustrated because she doesn't yet understand English sufficiently to follow classroom directions as well as peers)?

4. Could this problem be related to deprivation from an institutional background (e.g., the child is from an orphanage and has difficulty making decisions, is afraid of being on playground equipment, hoards food, or lacks basic social skills)?

Part II

Helping the Child at School

Chapter 4

Classroom Strategies for Parents and Teachers

Children adopted from abroad as infants or toddlers may go happily off to day care, preschool, or kindergarten with their same-age peers. Children adopted at ages 3 or 4 or beyond, however, may experience some difficulty as they transition from their adoption and new family to the more demanding world of preschool, elementary school, or even secondary school. They may be afraid and shy, unable to understand or speak the language, or lacking the cognitive, motor, and social skills necessary to interact successfully with their peers.

Of course, many children of intercountry adoption will be quite successful at school. Others, however, will struggle as they go up the grades. Although children of intercountry adoption are certainly at risk when compared with their peers, parents and teachers must remember that each child is a unique individual. Clearly, no assumptions can be made regarding the impact of intercountry adoption on any particular child in school!

As with any child, however, the key to successful performance begins in the classroom—with collaboration and cooperation between school personnel and parents. *Teachers can look to parents as the experts on their own child and parents can look to teachers as the experts on what children of the same age typically do.* Problems can often be overcome and the effects of initial difficulties lessened by careful attention from both parents and teachers to the unique needs of the child within the classroom. Of particular importance to academic success for children of intercountry adoption, then, are such factors as choosing the "right" school, teacher, or grade level, providing relevant information to the teacher, using positive adoption language, adapting lessons and assignments to accommodate for adoption, and preserving connections to the child's birth country.

※ CHOOSING A SCHOOL, TEACHER, AND GRADE LEVEL

To ensure the best experience possible for their child, parents are wise to search carefully for a supportive teacher with whom they can feel comfortable and a preschool or school setting that will accommodate the unique needs of their child. For young children, most working parents choose local preschool or day-care programs offered through churches or an employer or operated as a nearby business by an individual or company. When children reach school age, parents may enroll them in the local public school or in a private school, or they may opt to "home school." The choice of setting depends on individual preferences, religion, availability, and finances.

Local public schools usually have fully licensed teachers and typically offer a wide range of helpful services, including special education and English as a Second Language (ESL). They also may have a more diverse student body than private schools, helping children who are adopted transracially and transculturally to feel "less different." Class sizes, however, may be larger in public schools than in private schools. Private schools may offer the religious orientation parents prefer and smaller class sizes, but they are expensive and sometimes require parents to donate their time in service to the school. Moreover, private schools may not offer the resources, cultural diversity, special services, or fully licensed teachers available in public schools. Finally, parents who choose to home school are certainly able to give abundant individual attention to their children; however, they must realize that being both parent and teacher is an exhausting job! Additionally, opportunities for language and social stimulation are more readily available in a typical school setting than for home-schooled children, and not all children respond positively to academic correction and "tutoring" by a parent.

Regardless of whether or not parents choose to use a public or a private school, a careful search is still essential, particularly if they have not yet had any other children attend a school. Parents must be advocates for the needs of their children and teachers must remember that the parents have waited a long time for their child and have traveled many miles to make that child a part of their family. They have invested a great deal of emotional and physical energy and mean no disrespect to teachers and schools when they ask the following questions:

- What is the pupil–teacher ratio in the preschool or school? (The smaller the number of children assigned to a teacher the more likely the teacher will be able to give individual attention to each child.) How many teacher aides are available, what is their level of training, and how are they used?
- Have you taught children having English as a second language, children newly adopted from other countries, or children with disabilities before? (Some areas of the country have a large population of children whose families are new to the United States. These schools are likely to have greater cultural diversity and a higher concentration of children with English as a second language, and thus they may have special programs and teacher assistance available as the child learns English. Also, teachers who frequently work with children having disabilities or those in a multicultural environment may be more willing and able to adapt instruction to accommodate the unique needs of a diverse group of children.)
- May I observe in the classroom for a little while? (Teachers fostering a positive classroom climate are likely to be friendly with the children, look on the bright side of things, and actively teach children the proper way to behave rather than merely punishing misbehavior. Children in this type of classroom are productively engaged in learning and the teacher has the attitude that all children can learn and be successful in the classroom. In addition, some teachers have a highly structured classroom with children working at their desks, whereas others have quite "busy" classrooms with children sprawled on the floor or working independently. Some children will do better with structure and others will respond better to an environment with increased choices and responsibility.)
- May I bring my child in to meet you and see the classroom when no other children are there? (The child can see the classroom and the teacher without the distractions of others around. Additionally, the teacher can observe the reactions of the child to his or her new surroundings and can begin to gauge the child's readiness for learning in the classroom. Equally important, the parent can observe the teacher's ability to respond to and interact with the child.)

- What special services are available in the school when children are having difficulty? (Early intervention programs exist in many schools and communities to help young children who are developmentally delayed or at risk of school failure. In addition, special education services are guaranteed by law in all *public* schools to children who meet the eligibility criteria [see Chapter 6]. When parents choose to place their children in private schools, however, they must realize that the same special education services will not necessarily be available.)

- May I talk with a few parents of other children about the school? (Parents who are members of the parent–teacher organization might be helpful in giving information about the overall climate of the school; however, only parents of children who have been in a particular class can give insight on that classroom. Talking with several different families may help to eliminate bias if any parents are overly enthusiastic or critical about the school or its teachers.)

As parents search for the appropriate school placement for their child, they might also consider certain individual characteristics of their son or daughter. They may, for example, request testing, publicly or privately, to determine the child's grade level, although most schools prefer to place children in the grade that corresponds to their age level and give individual help as it is needed. When school-age children come to the United States during the middle of a school year, however, parents may wish to keep the child at home to adjust, beginning school the following fall even if this means the child may be one grade level behind his or her chronological-age peers. Moreover, the 3- to 4-year-old child who is physically small and socially immature for his or her chronological age may fare better if given time to catch up at home before entering day care or preschool. Similarly, the small, immature 5-year-old may be better placed in a preschool or junior kindergarten program than in kindergarten and the 6-year-old may be better placed in a kindergarten classroom rather than in first grade, particularly if language and concept skills are still delayed. As a matter of fact, parents sometimes change their child's birth date to a later year at the time of adoption to give the youngster additional months to adjust before entering school. By delaying school entry or lowering the grade level, parents and teachers may achieve a better "match" with the child's developmental age than by adhering to his or her chronological age placement.

Alternatively, the child who is tall or physically mature and who readily grasps new concepts may be best placed with same-age peers, with perhaps a translator or some additional assistance provided by a teacher, instructional aide, or peer tutor for language and concept development. Some schools offer multiage placements and "looping" that can be excellent arrangements for children of intercountry adoptions who need to be challenged. In looping arrangements, the same teacher stays with a group of children as they move up the grade levels. The kindergarten teacher, thus, becomes the child's first- and second-grade teacher, and so on. Looping allows the teacher to become well acquainted with the needs of the child and the child to become comfortable in an ongoing relationship with an important adult. Multiage classrooms typically blend two grade levels together, with two teachers and often one or more instructional assistants. Children enter the second–third-grade multiage classroom as second graders, for example, and have the same teachers the following year as third graders. As with looping, teachers, parents, and children have more than one year to get to know each other. Moreover, children requiring language stimulation or needing to develop missing concepts or social skills are exposed to better models through the older children in the multiage classroom and children who are "bossy" are not as likely to continue to be so in the face of pressure from older peers.

Without a doubt, choosing the "right" teacher and the proper grade placement is critical to a successful school experience. Teachers, however, must certainly take care not to assume automatically that children adopted from abroad beyond the age of 2, particularly those adopted from institutions, will have difficulty in the classroom. As a matter of fact, if teachers lower their expectations for these children, they may be inadvertently working against the parents' efforts to teach the child to "try" (Dellisanti, 1994). Moreover, for many children of intercountry adoption parents and teachers will want to "speed up" the child's rate of learning, *intensifying instruction* to build concepts and language as rapidly as the child can handle them.

As children go up the grades and have numerous teachers rather than just one, however, parents may find it increasingly difficult to communicate and establish a relationship with teachers at school. Nevertheless, parents can continue to advocate for their child's unique needs, through, for example, a guidance counselor, an assistant principal assigned to the child's grade level, or a grade-level team leader. Additionally, some parents find it helpful to request, whenever possible, that their child be placed in a classroom containing at least one other adopted child or a child of another nationality who immigrated to the United States to help remove the stigma of being "different" from their child. In fact, some parents report having moved so that their child can interact with others of the same ethnic or cultural heritage (Rojewski & Rojewski, 2001). Regardless of the grade level, parents will likely find it necessary to provide some information about their child's adoption to the teacher(s)—at least initially until the child is well adjusted at school.

❈ HOW MUCH INFORMATION SHOULD BE SHARED?

Many parents who adopt children are afraid that teachers and school professionals have misperceptions and prejudices about adoption (Dellisanti, 1994). Parents might believe, for example, that teachers see adoption as a "second best" way to form a family or that teachers think children who are adopted will automatically have difficulty learning and behaving in school. On the other hand, most teachers and school personnel are willing and even eager to work with parents, seeing them as authorities on their own children, but they are unable to do so effectively if they remain "uneducated" about adopted children. In addition, teachers have many different children in their classrooms, including many children with demanding behaviors and unique needs, and most want to do their best for *all* children in their class. Most experts on adoption encourage parents to share their child's adoptive status with teachers and to take the initiative to enhance the teacher's knowledge about adoption as a legitimate way to form a family (Gilman, 1992; Melina, 1998).

According to Melina (1998), a child's adoption is part of his or her social history, and schools need information on a child's social history in order to understand and meet the child's needs. For children adopted internationally as infants, parental disclosure of information may entail no more than that the children were born in a particular country and adopted by the parents as babies. This information is important to teachers to help them adapt assignments or handle questions asked by the other children as they arise. For example, without the knowledge that a child was born in Russia, a teacher might innocently ask the children to complete an activity such as "Find someone else in the class born in the same hospital (or town or state) as you." This is certainly an activity that a child of intercountry adoption is unlikely to complete successfully! Similarly, without advance information about a child's adoption and ways to handle comments made by other children, teachers may not have appropriate language to respond to public declarations such as "Tomorrow is my Happy 'Gotcha' (or Happy Adoption) Day" or to questions such as "So who's your *real* mother?"

Melina (1998) also encouraged parents to set an appointment to speak to teachers privately at the start of each school year asking that any information that is shared be held confidential. That is, teachers and other school professionals have a need to know about the child's adoptive status, but they have a responsibility to discuss that information only with other professionals who also have a need to know and only in private where others cannot overhear their discussion. Moreover, Melina suggested that parents share only information that the child already knows and inform teachers when they are being told something that the child does not yet know. In other words, much of the personal information about a child's adoption, his or her birth family, and so forth "belongs" to the child and parents, just like any sensitive information about a family such as income or lifestyle. Therefore, teachers and other school personnel should not "pry" by asking questions such as "Do you know who her mother is?" (Her mother is the person talking to the teacher at the moment!) or "Why was she put in the orphanage?" (This question isn't usually relevant for teaching the child!). Parents need not divulge information unless it is critical to the child's successful adjustment at school and in the best interest of the child for the teacher to know.

Parents, for example, need not tell teachers the specific facts they know about the preschool or school-age child's birth mother or the context of his or her placement in an orphanage. However, teachers will certainly be in a better position to help the child if they know that he or she was in an institutionalized environment prior to adoption. This *privileged information* will enable the teacher not only to adapt assignments as necessary but also to understand the child's lack of concepts and language or any unusual behaviors the child might exhibit. Without this important information, teachers and school psychologists might falsely attribute the child's lack of knowledge or language skills to lower cognitive ability. Similarly, without knowing about the child's years in an orphanage, the teacher might view the child who has no concept of personal possessions as a thief or the child with a sensory integration disorder who responds aggressively to touch as demonstrating misbehavior. Too, the guidance counselor or school psychologist will be unable to help the child deal with separation anxiety, grief, or loss or improve his or her self-esteem if they lack knowledge regarding the child's adoptive status.

As a matter of fact, Melina (1998) suggested that unless the child has obvious disabilities, parents should inform teachers they don't necessarily expect "special treatment" for their child. Nevertheless, parents should give teachers enough information to enable them to empathize and give extra attention to children of intercountry adoption as it is needed. For example, the child may be adopted transracially, or he or she may be aware of siblings still in the birth country and casually mention these during a class discussion. If teachers do not know about these siblings or if they are unsure regarding how to handle questions posed by classmates about why their friend differs in physical appearance from his or her parents, they can quickly become confused and unable to respond effectively to comments from the child's peers.

Younger children may feel special as their parents share important information with their teachers. In fact, some parents even arrange to give special presentations in their child's classroom about adoption or about the child's birth country. As children get older, however, they may prefer not to appear different from their peers. Consequently, children who are adopted may request that their parents not share information about their adoption with teachers, and special presentations in the classroom certainly become taboo. If the child's adoption has been discussed openly within the family for many years, hopefully the child will have the skills to handle questions or comments from peers positively on his or her own. If the child does not have the skills, however, parents may still need to inform the teacher(s) regarding the youngster's adoption, but they should do so only after first telling the child about their intentions. Without knowledge of the child's adoption, teachers cannot be expected to adapt assignments as necessary or ascribe inattention, withdrawal, or irritability to the "normal" process of dealing with adoption-related issues.

Obviously, children of intercountry adoption may come to the preschool or school before they have mastered English or fully adjusted to their new surroundings. Many will come with no previous experience with "formal" school settings such as the preschool or elementary school and most will lack the alphabetic and numeric concepts usually attained by American children prior to kindergarten. The parents of a child adopted internationally at 3 or 4 years of age or older almost always will need to alert preschool or school personnel to their child's adoption. Teachers certainly have a need to know how long the child has been in the United States so that ESL or translating services can be offered if possible (see Chapter 5). Additionally, these children may not be able to talk to parents or counselors about past abuse that they might have suffered until sufficient English develops and they feel comfortable in the new home, school, and classroom. According to Dellisanti (1994), for example, "Children who have been institutionalized . . . have not had a chance to develop what is considered a normal range of emotions, let alone a vocabulary and a sense of entitlement to respect and safety, to allow themselves to describe past experiences" (p. 65). Teachers, social workers, and school counselors may need time to locate individuals having expertise with the child's language or culture, particularly if the child is having a difficult adjustment to the home and school.

Moreover, children adopted internationally and transracially will most likely be visibly different from their parents; therefore, questions from peers are sure to come more quickly for these youngsters, particularly in less diverse rural areas of the country, than for other children of intercountry adoption who look similar to their parents. Children from about ages 7 to 11 are generally accepted by their dominant-culture peers; however, as they enter secondary schools they may experience rejection from either the dominant-culture peers, peers from their own ethnic group, or both (Steinberg & Hall, 2000). Moreover, some older children may be embarrassed over the interracial composition of their own families (Dellisanti, 1994) and some younger children, whether or not they have been adopted, may make confused assumptions about adoption and racial or ethnic membership such as the following:

- All brown people are adopted.
- All Chinese females are adopted.
- All Koreans are adopted.
- All interracial families are adoptive families.
- If you are the same color as your parents, you weren't adopted.
- All children born in another country are adopted. (adapted from Steinberg & Hall, 2000, p. 229)

Too, parents of children from intercountry adoptions are often older than are the parents of their children's peers. Such a visible age difference may precipitate comments like, "Isn't he *really* your *grandfather*?" Unless parents have carefully explained to teachers and other school professionals about their child's adoption and helped them to develop positive language to handle such encounters, the self-esteem of vulnerable children can be easily affected.

※ USING POSITIVE ADOPTION LANGUAGE

Parents differ regarding when and how they discuss adoption with their child and how they refer to individuals from their child's past. For children adopted beyond infancy, parents and teachers certainly cannot simply deny the past years of the child's life. Questions about the past will inevitably arise, however, regardless of the child's age at the time of adoption, and parents will need to be prepared to answer these questions in a positive manner. In addition, teachers and other school personnel need positive adoption language in order to support the child as he or she deals with adoption-related issues or encounters questions, comments, or teasing from peers.

As children enter preschool or kindergarten, for example, the child who is adopted from China, like Olivia, might gleefully tell her adoption story. The other children may innocently ask, "Why don't you look like your mommy and daddy?" or "Where is your *real* mommy?" Her parents may tell her that "a real mommy is the person who loves you and takes care of you all your life." Although this may be believable and comforting to the adopted child, other children still may not understand why their friend wasn't born to her mother. Teachers must be prepared to help all children in the classroom understand that families are formed in many different and wonderful ways.

Parents and teachers can help children at this age by emphasizing that families are people who love each other and take care of each other. They can reinforce the notion through pictures, videos, stories, or discussion that there are many different types of families, with children living with one parent, two parents, stepparents, stepbrothers and stepsisters, grandparents, aunts, uncles, and so forth. All of these types of families are indeed *real* families because they are composed of people who love each other and care for one another. They can also illustrate that family members may or may not resemble each other and model for children a respect for individual differences including physical appearance and disabilities. Additionally, many wonderful books are available to share with preschoolers and young elementary age children about families and about adoption from various countries (see Appendix B) including the following:

- *Beginnings: How Families Come to Be*, by Virginia Kroll
- *Families Are Different*, by Nina Pellegrini
- *When You Were Born in Korea*, by Brian Boyd (Korea)
- *Good Morning Vietnam, Good Afternoon, USA*, by Anna Hudson (Vietnam)
- *I Love You Like Crazy Cakes*, by Rose Lewis (China)
- *Mommy Far, Mommy Near*, by Carol Antoinette Peacock (China)
- *Adoption Is Okay*, by Sylvia Rohde (Russia)
- *Look Who's Adopted*, by Michael S. Taheri and James F. Orr (Famous people who have been adopted.)

Most experts agree that a parent's or teacher's choice of words conveys much to children about what they believe (Melina, 1998). Hopefully, parents and teachers will model acceptance and positive, rather than negative, attitudes about adoption. According to Meese (1999), expressing tough concepts through positive language is an important skill for all teachers. For example, teachers and other school professionals must take care not to give the impression that only biological parents are "real" parents. *The real parents are the ones who are parenting the child!* Similarly, teachers and school personnel must refrain from speaking about "natural" parents as if the people who adopted the child are not "natural" or "real" parents. There is nothing "unnatural" about adoption—it is simply another way to form a family, just as is giving birth to a child or blending a family together through a second or a third marriage. People who adopt their children are not "like a mother or father" to their children; rather, they *are* the mother and father of their children! Thus, teachers might choose to use the following important language as they handle "adoption" questions and comments posed by children in their classes:

- Say "parent(s)," "mother," or "father" when referring to people who have adopted children. (Do *not* say "adoptive mother/father/parent" or "like a mother/father/parent." Teachers don't ordinarily refer to parents of other children as their "blood-related mom or dad," therefore, to add the term *adoptive* unnecessarily creates a difference that need not be emphasized.)
- Say "birth parent," "birth mother," or "birth father" when referring to the biological parent(s), *or,*
- Say "biological parent," "biological mother," or "biological father" when referring to biological parent(s) (Do *not* say "natural" or "real" parent/mother/father!)

- Say "the birth mother could not take care of any baby" rather than "the birth mother could not take care of (*Name of child*)" in order to prevent sending the message that something was "wrong" with the child that kept the birth mother from caring for him or her.
- Say the birth mother "made an adoption plan" or "made a plan so her child could have parents" instead of "She gave up (or gave away) her child." Young children can easily become frightened that they can be "given away."

Knowing positive adoption language in advance will enable teachers to respond to questions asked by other children and support the child who is adopted when situations arise. Assume, for example, that a child asks a question such as "If Olivia comes from China, why can't she speak Chinese?" The teacher with advance preparation might reply "Lots of people come to the United States and they learn to speak English. Olivia was born in China but now she's an American citizen." Or, suppose a child asks, "Why doesn't Jennifer live with her real mom in Romania?" This difficult question can be answered briefly, but honestly: "Jennifer is living with her real mom—here in America" or "Sometimes mothers give birth to their babies but they aren't able to take care of a baby. They want their baby to have a family to be safe and loved in, so Jennifer has a family just like yours and mine."

As children advance through the grades and develop a deeper understanding of adoption, positive language continues to be essential for use by teachers and other school personnel as they model acceptance for all children including the child who is adopted. Teachers, for example, can continue to help youngsters see the multifaceted nature of families in today's society, including both single-parent and two-parent families who have adopted some or all of their children. They can also demonstrate tolerance for diversity (e.g., physical appearance or size, disabilities, cultural or ethnic heritage, adoption, etc.) in the classroom and they can insist on respect for individual differences rather than permitting teasing. Numerous opportunities exist within the curriculum for introducing adoption as a legitimate topic for study including an examination of immigration in social studies or discussing theatrical productions or works of literature such as *Annie* or *Anne of Green Gables*. Nevertheless, as older children comprehend that adoption also means relinquishment and loss, teachers and parents can point to famous people (e.g., the actor Ted Danson) who have been adopted or provide the children with additional reading material to answer their increasingly complex questions. Good books for preteens and teenagers, for example, include (see Appendix B):

- *Why Didn't She Keep Me? Answers to the Question Every Adopted Child Asks*, by Barbara Burlingham-Brown
- *The Face in the Mirror: Teenagers and Adoption*, by Marion Crook
- *Who Am I? . . . And Other Questions of Adopted Kids*, by Charlene C. Giannetti.

Teachers can provide informative books for youngsters to read and they can be wonderful models of positive language and acceptance of diversity. Sometimes, however, they can overlook the subtle, or not-so-subtle, impact of daily activities, discussions, and assignments on the child who is adopted. Frequently, the very language used during instruction can, unbeknownst to the teacher, precipitate memories and discomfort for children who are adopted: grouping math problems or spelling words into "families" based on similar appearances, for example (Maskew, 1999). In order to prevent the child who is adopted from standing out from his or her peers, some activities may need to be adapted.

�֍ ADAPTING LESSONS AND ASSIGNMENTS

Although parents realize that an entire class cannot be modified just to accommodate one child, all too often teachers forget in the hurried world of the classroom that some assignments and activities are painful, difficult, or even impossible for the child who is adopted—especially for the child of intercountry adoption. Making a Mother's Day card, for example, can bring about painful feelings of loss, not only for children who are adopted, but also for children who have lost a parent through death, divorce, or foster care placement. Simple adaptations to these activities can make a big difference both for the comfort of children who are adopted and for their parents. These adaptations, however, should be used routinely as a matter of choice for *all* children in the classroom rather than just singling out children who are adopted and telling them to change the assignment. Children having single or divorced parents, children living in foster care arrangements, and children living with others than their parents can also profit from sensitive adaptations to typical assignments. *When all children can choose from a list of possible options, everyone is "safe" and no one will stand out as different.*

For example, a typical activity in the preschool or elementary school classroom is the preparation of a "Super Star" or "Who's Who?" or "Student of the Week"-type bulletin board. Children are spotlighted in turn on this bulletin board and asked to bring in pictures of themselves, their pets, and their families. A frequent request is to bring in a baby picture for placement on this bulletin board. Although some children of intercountry adoption will indeed have baby pictures, many of these children will not. The earliest picture for most of them will be at age 2, 3, 4, or up. Moreover, often the earliest picture available is of the child in the orphanage in clothing, hairstyle, and surroundings that may be less than flattering and completely different than in the other children's pictures. Asking all children in the classroom to bring in their favorite pictures of themselves, regardless of their age in the photographs, is a simple adaptation that will give all of the children a safe option (Meese, 1999).

Another frequent assignment in the elementary grades is to produce a timeline of one's life. Teachers might ask children to place pictures on the timeline to illustrate one significant event for each year in their lives from birth until the present. Typical examples offered by teachers are to use a picture shortly after birth, a picture of the child's first steps, or a picture from a first or second birthday party. Again, children of intercountry adoption are not likely to have pictures such as these from the earliest years of their lives. Additionally, for some children, basic information about their birth may be missing altogether and the first few years of their lives may be mostly "blank" pages with little information provided to their parents by orphanage directors. Moreover, children may not want to share the information that they do remember or that may have been provided to them and their parents.

Again, simple adaptations can easily be made for this activity. For example, teachers can give all children the choice of using a photograph or drawing pictures or combining photographs and drawings to illustrate an event for each year of life. Children from intercountry adoption, then, can safely draw pictures of themselves for years having no photographs. They can draw themselves as a baby or they can draw a picture of anything about which they and their parents have been given information—such as having chicken pox at age 3! Alternatively, teachers can simply ask all children to make a timeline for the "best year" or the "best day" in their life containing at least six or seven pictures or photos to illustrate the day's or year's events in sequence. In this way, children of intercountry adoption can safely pick an age or time for which they have many photographs and many "events" to chronicle.

Sometimes teachers involve the entire class in an "adoption" project. Children work as a group to raise money to "adopt a whale," or "adopt the bay," or "adopt a park," or "adopt an animal in a zoo." According to Dellisanti (1994), such casual use of the term *adoption*, although not meant to cause offense, can easily wound children who are adopted. In other words, if we continue to pay for the whale or the bay or the park or the zoo animal, it will be "ours"; if not, someone else can own it. This cavalier approach trivializes adoption and sends the message to the young child and to his or her peers that an adoption lasts only as long as parents are willing to "pay" for the child. For older children of intercountry adoption who might have overheard adults asking their parents "how much it cost" to adopt from Russia or China or Romania, the anxiety raised by such a project can be overwhelming. To avoid sending such a negative message teachers are encouraged instead to select terms such as "*save* a whale," or "*save* the bay," or "*sponsor* a park," or "*sponsor* a zoo animal" whenever possible.

Writing an autobiography, interviewing an older family member, constructing a family history, inviting grandparents to the class, making a family tree, and examining family genetics are additional assignments likely to cause difficulty for many children who are adopted or who are in alternative living arrangements away from parents. Children of intercountry adoption, however, are likely to have added problems associated with such assignments. Again, adaptations to these activities can easily be offered as options for all children. Regardless of the adaptations, however, teachers and parents must remember that these assignments might precipitate questions, fears, inattention, and even misbehavior as children are compelled to consider adoption-related issues. Teachers, school counselors, and parents, therefore, will need to be prepared to handle these questions and fears in a sensitive, but positive, manner.

Autobiographies

Teachers often require students to write an autobiography or to construct a poster that depicts the milestones in the student's life. Many simple adaptations for autobiographies or similar assignments can easily be made. For example, teachers can allow children to write about any events in their life that they might want to share. Teachers can set a criterion for a specific number of events and then allow children to choose what to include rather than requiring that they start with birth and write about every significant event each year until the present. Children of intercountry adoption certainly cannot provide specific details for important events from birth onward, and they may not want to share details about some of the events they do remember! Some will want to write about their adoption and trip home, and others will not.

As an alternative, teachers can ask children to write about or illustrate a particular year or "big event" in their life. Or, teachers can ask children to write a full autobiography, but not ask children to read these aloud. Moreover, if teachers do choose to require a full autobiography or a "life poster," they should refrain from placing these on a bulletin board or classroom wall. In this way, children of intercountry adoption do not have to reveal information they would rather not share with others and they do not have to face answering questions about why they did not include certain information other children included as a matter of course.

Interviewing an Older Family Member and Constructing the Family History

Teachers frequently ask children to interview someone in their family from a previous generation. Such an assignment might be used in social studies, for example, to enable children to obtain a firsthand account of life many years ago or in English or language arts as a part of a writing assignment to create a family history. Although many children of intercountry adoption have grandparents or older aunts and uncles they may willingly interview, many others adopted by older parents will not. Moreover, as children grow older, having to interview someone from a previous generation, particularly to construct a family history, opens up questions regarding which family. Children of intercountry adoption, of course, may have limited or no information regarding their birth family and certainly most have no opportunity to interview someone from their birth family given the distances involved. Even when the child has met his or her birth family, the expense and difficulty of contacting these family members abroad will most likely be prohibitive.

Teachers can adapt this assignment by permitting children to interview someone from a previous generation—period. This individual could be a family friend, someone in the family's church, or a neighbor, and not necessarily a grandparent or another elderly family member. The choice is left to each child and his or her parents with the focus of the interview on obtaining the individual's life history or an account of life in the "olden days" or some other type of information. Similarly, children can be given the choice of constructing their own family history or that of another family. Children who are adopted might choose to construct their own family's history, that of their birth family, or a combination of the two, or they might choose to write a history of a friend's family. Again, several options will provide safe choices for all children in the classroom regardless of their life circumstances.

Grandparents

Schools often have activities grandparents are encouraged to attend. Family nights, during which children give special presentations, and "grandparent" days on which a child's grandparents visit the classroom or have lunch with their grandson or granddaughter are two such occasions. Grandparents today are also frequently invited to enter elementary school classrooms as helpers or volunteers or to read to children and listen to children read to them.

Teachers, of course, must realize that today's grandparents often live many miles away from their grandchildren; therefore, some children, regardless of whether or not they are adopted, may be unable to have their grandparents present for these activities. Many children of intercountry adoption will have grandparents in the United States, either many miles away or locally. Many others, however, will have older parents whose own parents are now deceased. Sometimes older parents who have adopted internationally arrange for a "surrogate" set of grandparents through willing friends, a local church, adoption agency, or cultural group in order to provide their child contact with an older generation or a connection to his or birth country. Teachers can give all children in the classroom the option to bring a grandparent or an "older friend" to participate in activities whenever appropriate. Thus, all children, adopted or not, can bring an elderly friend with their parents' assistance and permission when grandparents are not available.

Making a Family Tree

The construction of a family tree can help children learn about their "roots." As a social studies project or writing assignment in English class, this activity is an enjoyable way for children to personalize their learning. For children who are adopted, however, this assignment can also prompt questions regarding "whose family." Some children will want to construct the branches of their family tree using their own parents and their family members. Others might choose to create the family tree using their birth parents and birth family. Still others might choose to place their birth parents at the root of the tree and construct the branches of the tree by using their family.

Teachers can validate each of these ideas by sharing samples in advance, of course without singling out any particular children, and they can encourage all children to produce their family tree however they deem appropriate. Teachers, of course, must remember that children of intercountry adoption may have little or no information regarding their birth family. In addition, they must remember that any child who is adopted or any child not living with both parents— regardless of the reason(s)—is likely to feel some discomfort when asked to construct a family tree or to complete an equivalent type of assignment. Insisting that children complete the tree with only the family or only the birth family may produce embarrassment and resistance. Allowing children to include what they feel comfortable sharing on their family tree is the safest option. Creating a family circle illustrating the various individuals who provide love and support to the child may be even safer.

Tracing Genetic Roots

As children enter upper elementary school or the secondary schools and learn basic biology, they are often requested to trace their genetic roots. Having children determine how they might have inherited their blue eyes or red hair is an intriguing and interesting assignment for most children—unless they are adopted. Children of intercountry adoption, of course, may have absolutely no information regarding their birth mother or birth father and they probably do not have a picture of these individuals. Asking children of intercountry adoption to complete this impossible assignment is likely to precipitate tears or complaints at home, particularly when the child does not look like his or her parents.

Again, easy adaptations can be offered for all children in the classroom. Teachers can simply allow children to choose to use their family or their birth family, for example. If they have pictures or information about their birth heritage, they might choose this option from a sense of pride. On the other hand, if children are lacking information about the birth family or are uncomfortable about their birth country, they might choose to figure out how their blue eyes or some other personal characteristic such as height might have been passed through their own family.

Two safer options, however, remove the choice of family versus birth family. With prior notification to administrators and parents, teachers can simply pair a boy and a girl in the class and ask them to determine likely eye or hair colors for potential offspring. Or, teachers can construct case scenarios containing fictional family members or fictional "spouses." Students can then determine the likelihood of various characteristics in the children of the fictional family or in their own children given the fictional spouse.

Regardless of the type of assignment—tracing genetics, constructing a family history or family tree, writing an autobiography, or making a timeline of one's life—teachers will need to plan appropriate ways to "grade" the products. Often teachers construct rubrics for such assignments, requiring a certain type or quantity of information be included and attention to details of correct grammar and spelling. Certainly, the mechanical elements of these projects (e.g., spelling, capitalization, grammar, punctuation, neatness) can be required of all students to the best of their ability, granted that some children who are newly adopted internationally may have limited English skills! The more "subjective" portion of the rubric, however, must be written flexibly. Teachers, for example, can easily "undo" the safe options they have provided for children if they inadvertently place on the rubric for an autobiography a requirement such as "states birth place" or a requirement on a rubric for a family tree "identifies father's parents and identifies mother's parents."

❊ BIRTH COUNTRY CONNECTIONS

Although parents disagree regarding the benefits and importance of emphasizing their child's cultural heritage (Rojewski & Rojewski, 2001), parents of children from intercountry adoptions often try to preserve a connection with their child's birth country and ethnic heritage, particularly when the child is younger. They often do so, however, with the dawning realization that they do not really know what it is to be a member of their child's cultural or ethnic group, nor will they ever fully know (Rojewski & Rojewski, 2001; Steinberg & Hall, 2000). Nevertheless, they may, for example, attend cultural events such as the ballet or a concert when touring groups from the child's birth country are in their town. Or, they may eat at ethnic restaurants, take classes in the child's language, and locate churches or befriend families nearby having ties to their child's country of origin. Many adoption organizations also periodically host cultural events or cultural camps featuring food, music, crafts, and holiday celebrations from particular countries of interest (see Appendix A). Families for Russian and Ukrainian Adoption (FRUA) and Families with Children from China (FCC) are but two of many organizations sponsoring such cultural events locally throughout the United States.

As children age, they may indeed enjoy attending cultural events, eating at ethnic restaurants, and purchasing clothing, dolls, or other items from their birth country. They may wish to bring into school folk costumes, instruments, toys, or books their parents obtained for them to share from their country of birth. Other children, though, may resist these reminders about their birth country as they grow older, preferring instead to look and behave as their peers do rather than to stand out as "different." Moreover, some children of intercountry adoption actively resist connections to their birth country from the moment they arrive in the United States, appearing tense and frightened, for example, around speakers of their native language.

Regardless of a child's interest in his or her birth country, parents and teachers must take care to promote a sense of pride in the youngster's heritage, especially because many of these children will have so little information regarding their birth family. Consequently, the birth country may take on the role of "birth family" and evoke a strong sense of identification for some children (Schoettle, 2000). Coupled with that sense of pride, however, must be a tempering dose of "realism" so that the child does not unrealistically glorify his or her country of birth.

Additionally, parents and teachers must be keenly aware of how all children, including children of intercountry adoption, are learning about their or their family's countries of origin, particularly in rural areas where cultural or ethnic diversity is limited (Rojewski & Rojewski, 2001; Schoettle, 2000). According to Schoettle, "Just as children's concept of themselves as adoptees is greatly influenced by how adoption is viewed by those around them, their perception of their birth country, and consequently their birth family, can be impacted by the opinions and statements of others" (p. 1). Thus, teachers must consider, for example in social studies classes, how the child's birth country is presented in books, movies, and discussions. Are attitudes of teachers and peers positive or negative toward Russia, China, or Korea? Do children make jokes or teasing comments in the hallways about "slanted eyes" or use derogatory language about countries such as these? How will children react when they view a movie about the Korean War, about Stalin, about communist China, or about the cold war with the former Soviet Union countries? How will children react if they see a television report about babies "sold" from Romania and bring this information to class? How will they respond to television or newspaper accounts of poverty or alcoholism or HIV in their birth country? How will they react to seeing pictures of children still in orphanages or living on the streets of Bucharest or Moscow? For children who are adopted internationally, mixed feelings of embarrassment, shame, and guilt can easily overcome any sense of pride in their heritage unless teachers and parents help children to see that all countries, including the United States, have both positive and negative attributes (Schoettle, 2000).

Similarly, Dellisanti (1994) urged teachers not to focus on the "trappings" of various cultures such as food, clothing, and music. Such characteristics highlight the differences among countries rather than the universal needs and feelings of all people. Although learning about food, clothing, music, and holidays can be positive and interesting, Dellisanti (1994) suggested that the sharing of these activities alone can present a country as "quaint" or as "wonderfully old-fashioned." Because no country is completely good or completely bad, children adopted internationally must be permitted to grieve the loss of their homeland due to very unfortunate circumstances. They must also learn that most people in the birth country are still people just like in their own families who do care about their children whether the children are able to remain with their birth families or not.

The United States is a diverse country culturally and ethnically and the children in today's classrooms are quite diverse. Therefore, teachers must present accurate and current information about other countries and remain sensitive to the multicultural nature of their classrooms—regardless of whether or not the classroom contains children of intercountry adoptions. Nevertheless, some special suggestions to help teachers having children who are adopted internationally in the classroom include the following:

- Examine your own cultural or ethnic stereotypes and beliefs (e.g., Do you expect Olivia to do well in math because she is from China? Do you expect all children, regardless of their color or background, to do well in school?)

- Resist the temptation to insist that the child from China (or Russia or Korea or Romania, etc.) must always focus on his or her birth country when completing projects and reports. Children like Jennifer, Laura, and Olivia may or may not be interested in the topic or want to be the "class expert" on their birth country. They should have the same choice as any other child in the classroom!

- Remember that holidays and other special occasions, when celebrated in the traditions of the birth country, can sometimes provoke memories of the birth family in children of intercountry adoption.

- Portray both the "good" points and the "bad" points about all countries, including our own, objectively and fairly, rather than emphasizing certain ones so that they appear more important or dramatic than others.

- Focus on the idea that most people in other countries are just people like ourselves, wanting the best for their families, regardless of what their governments and leaders do.

❀ CONCLUSION

Many children of intercountry adoptions are likely to adjust and be successful in school. Many others, however, are at risk of school failure, particularly if they spent years in institutionalized settings. Teachers and parents can work together to minimize the effects of early deprivation and help these children learn and remain in the regular classroom. When teachers are carefully selected and informed about a child's adoption, they can empathize and understand the child's performance or behavior better than when they are unaware of his or her adoption. Moreover, sensitivity on the parts of teachers and other school professionals to the impact of adoption language and routine assignments on the social and emotional life of children who are adopted can help smooth "trouble spots" for these youngsters. Teachers can "interpret" adoption to other students when questions arise by using positive adoption language and they can foster acceptance by modeling respect for individual differences and multiple types of families. In addition, typical assignments such as timelines and autobiographies can easily be adapted to allow safe choices for all children—those who are and are not living with their parents as well as those who are adopted. Offering a choice gives children of intercountry adoption a legitimate way to participate successfully when they lack basic information about their birth family, birthplace, and birth history. Finally, teachers can work with parents to help preserve healthy connections to the child's birth country by acknowledging both the "good" and the "bad" in all countries and by emphasizing the similarity of all people in today's global society.

Chapter 5

Language, Learning, and Limited English Proficiency

Language is an essential tool for all children. Without language, children are unable to think, communicate with others, or regulate their own behavior (Vygotsky, 1978). For children having no physical or neurological difficulties affecting their speech, as well as good hearing and adequate cognitive ability, language learning occurs steadily from birth through the elementary years. Although the most rapid period of language growth takes place from birth until about age 5, children continue to develop and refine their language skills during middle childhood and throughout adolescence, regardless of which language they are learning (Bernstein & Tiegerman-Farber, 1997).

Language learning also occurs in a predictable developmental sequence; however, the rate of learning and the time at which particular skills are acquired varies greatly from child to child. For example, most children "coo" (e.g., repeat the same sound over and over such as "ooooo") and "babble" (e.g., string together syllables like "baba" and "dodo"), beginning to use the sounds and intonations of the language they hear around them, between birth and age 6 months. Most will say their first words in their native language somewhere between 12 and 18 months of age. During the preschool years, a child's language grows rapidly from one- or two-word simple sentences to language that is fairly complex by age 5, with most preschoolers, regardless of the language spoken, imitating others, asking questions, expressing their needs verbally, and answering simple questions (Bernstein & Tiegerman-Farber, 1997). According to Brown (1975), language learning for English-speaking children during the preschool years includes the following:

- Expanding vocabulary rapidly to label familiar people, objects, and actions
- Using a variety of sentence types (e.g., "I want the blue fruit juice"; "We went way up in the airplane"; "She had to go home because she was bad"; "If I pick up my toys, I'll get to hear a story"; When are we going?")
- Referring to self and others with pronouns (e.g., "mine, they, ours, theirs," etc.)
- Using question words (e.g., "Who, what, when, where, why, how") and negative constructions (e.g., "She won't/can't go")
- Using various word forms such as plurals (e.g., "ducks"), past tense verbs (e.g., "went" or "jumped"), the verb "to be" (e.g., "is, am, was, were, are"), articles (e.g., "the, a"), contractions (e.g., "I'm playing"), and prepositions (e.g., "under, on, in," etc.).

By the time American children enter kindergarten, then, they frequently have a vocabulary of 10,000 or more words and they have mastered the basic syntax (i.e., the way words are ordered in sentences) of the language. As children progress through elementary school, they continue to add new vocabulary and refine their language skills. They begin to understand and use jokes and figurative language (e.g., "He hit the roof") and to comprehend increasingly complex sentences (Bernstein & Tiegerman-Farber, 1997).

Although children continue to learn language throughout their preschool years, Locke (1993) suggests that the first 2 years of life are the critical periods for language development. Children who "miss" these critical stages for language acquisition may struggle throughout their lives and many may never catch up. Unfortunately, children of intercountry adoption, particularly those from institutionalized environments, are indeed at risk for missing these crucial developmental stages. In overcrowded orphanages having high ratios of children to staff and few educated caregivers, adequate language models are rare. So deprived is the level of language stimulation in some orphanages that Federici (2000) asserted children sometimes do not even learn their native language, but rather develop an "institutional language" combining gibberish and babbling. Moreover, children in orphanages often have few toys, little opportunity to explore the environment, restricted interactions with adults that primarily focus on the "business" of using the toilet, dressing, or eating, and no need to make decisions in a world that is completely structured for them (Federici, 1998; Hough, 2000). In short, they have little motivation to develop the range of language skills that are normally used by preschoolers as they engage in social interactions taking place naturally within families such as reading stories, requesting help to zip a jacket, playing a game, or asking for a snack.

As a matter of fact, Gindis (2000) reported that language delays are the most common diagnosis found in the medical records of children adopted beyond the age of 3 from orphanages. Additionally, he maintained that Russian physicians often mean unintelligible speech, limited vocabulary, and poor oral language comprehension when they place the label "developmental language delay" in a child's records. Of course, children placed in institutions abroad share many interacting factors initially placing them at risk for language delays and perhaps even resulting in such a label. These include low birth weight, poor pre- and postnatal health care, inadequate nutrition, maternal alcohol or other substance abuse, and chronic or acute middle ear infections (e.g., otitis media). Such risk factors, when combined with the lack of attention and stimulation given by caregivers, are likely to compound the problem of language development for many children once they arrive in an orphanage.

Most researchers following children who have been adopted from institutionalized environments during the last decade indicate that these children do frequently exhibit persistent speech and language delays (Groze & Ileana, 1996; Miller & Hendrie 2000; Price, 2000). Hough (2000), for example, reported that 55% to 60% of the children arriving in the United States from eastern European countries will have difficulty with speech and language. She also stated that 40% to 50% will learn English easily; however, their parents are often surprised at the difficulty these children have later on in school—despite an apparent fluency and ease in acquiring English. *The aforementioned statements are certainly not meant to imply that every child of intercountry adoption will have language delays or later difficulty learning in school; however, parents and school personnel must be aware that these youngsters are indeed at risk even after they acquire their second language.*

✳ ACQUIRING A SECOND LANGUAGE

Some parents of intercountry adoption may speak their child's language, whereas others may enroll in classes to learn the language in an attempt to preserve and expand it for their child (Alperson, 2001; Rojewski & Rojewski, 2001). These parents believe that the only way to become a family demonstrating true connections and respect for a child's birth country is through speaking his or her first language in the home. Most, however, learn only the basic vocabulary needed for travel in the birth country and for early interactions with their new son or daughter. Sometimes, even after arrival home, communication takes place at least initially through a translator. More often than not, however, initial communications occur via pointing to items in simple picture dictionaries, through gestures, pantomime, or facial expressions, and by speaking English normally in the home. Parents also find that exposure to other children of the same age hastens language learning for their child.

According to Gindis (1997), most children of intercountry adoption will lose their first language swiftly within the first 3 to 6 months, and certainly within the first year, after arrival in their new home. When these children no longer hear their first language and have no motivation or support for using it, they usually begin to acquire their new language. A few children, adopted at the same time as others or adopted as members of a sibling group, may retain their language somewhat longer, but ultimately they too will lose their native language without daily exposure to it. As Gindis (2000) stated, language is a function that will continue to exist only as long as it is used; therefore, children either "use it or lose it" (p. 92).

Children usually lose their first language, however, far faster than they gain their new one. As children begin to internalize the sounds, words, and rhythm of their new language, at first they may find English easier to listen to than to speak, and thus they may remain silent as they observe their new environment. They may also understand much of what parents or teachers are saying about them to others even though they are unable to respond for themselves! During this period of initial language loss and new language acquisition, children also may demonstrate temper tantrums and behavior problems related to frustration over their inability to comprehend their new language and surroundings and to communicate with important others. Such feelings are certainly understandable. As Maskew (1999) stated, children of intercountry adoption have just experienced profound changes in their lives, yet they are not able to tell others about their feelings or needs. Learning language, therefore, is crucial for the successful adjustment of these children at home and in school in their first year after adoption (Gindis, 2000).

For example, my daughter, Katie, adopted at age 4½ from an orphanage in Russia, was initially frustrated with our inability to articulate Russian words. She would take my face in her hands and attempt to push it into the proper position to form words such as "truck" (pronounced "groosaveek") in Russian! She was also frustrated with her own inability to understand and communicate with my husband and me—resorting to temper tantrums, gestures, and a "frozen" silence.

Even while still in Russia, however, Katie demonstrated an understanding that we spoke a different language and she showed an interest in learning how to communicate. She would point, for example, to my eyes or to her new baby doll and repeat "eye" or "baby" while nodding her head affirmatively and saying "da" (i.e., yes) after she heard and pronounced each word. Although Katie spoke primarily Russian during her first 2 to 3 weeks home, she rapidly entered a period during which she would gaze at herself in her bedroom mirror and speak what sounded like gibberish—no longer the Russian sounds she had when she arrived, but not yet English sounds either. Then rapidly her language exploded as illustrated by the following language samples that I recorded:

- At 1 month home, Katie labeled objects and actions—"Katie Sveta sleeping, sleeping," "Go big Smile store" (her name for WalMart), "Pick green beans."

- At 2 months home, she asked questions with inflections such as "Full?" and "Almost all gone?" She also asserted her own ideas ("Ice cream, good idea!") and used negations (Saying "Not a good idea" while shaking her her head from side to side and holding her foot over the cat's water dish).

- At 3 months home, Katie used simple sentences with prepositions and the personal pronoun "I" such as "I have to (or I want to) go to the store" and "I see a big helicopter way up there!"

- At 4 months home, she used imperatives ("Put your hand in your pocket!"), pronouns ("Our family, my Mama and Papa"), more complex sentences ("Long time ago, we came from Russia. We got a cake at the grocery story. In Russia, we no have one"), and contractions ("I'm not sure"). She also began to demonstrate an awareness of individual sounds within the English language (exclaiming "Look! My tongue goes way up here . . . /l/").

- At 5 months home, Katie used "because" ("Mama fuss Katie Sveta because Papa fuss Mama!") and during the sixth and seventh months home, Katie engaged in teasing conversations such as "You are maya doshka" (Dad saying "You are my daughter") to which Katie responded, "No papa, not maya doshka. Not in America!"
- By the end of her eighth month home, Katie was able to have conversations such as "Sorry, Mom. I just needed a kiss" (waking me up at night), "I was afraid in my room" (I responded with "Why?"), "The rain was blowing hard outside." Or, at another time when asked, "What are you doing?" Katie replied "I'm pretending to be a bride. I want to get a new long dress for my Barbie so Barbie can be a bride, too."

Obviously, the language development of one child, although illustrative, is not representative of all children of intercountry adoption. Nevertheless, most parents are just as surprised and delighted as I was that their children so quickly and easily learn to speak English. As a matter of fact, Maskew (1999) stated that children of intercountry adoption quickly mimic their parents' clichés (i.e., "Hold your horses") or inappropriate expressions from videos or television, sometimes using them at embarrassing moments much like a U.S.-born toddler might do! Such language learning, however, takes place in a *social-conversational context* quite different than the academic environment of school. Parents often become dismayed and confused when their seemingly "English-fluent" child encounters difficulty on school entry.

Unfortunately, most of the research regarding the school performance of children learning English as a second language has examined bilingual children—that is, children of immigrant parents who come to the United States and retain their native language to some degree. Usually, these children have already attained skills in their native language appropriate for their developmental level. Thus, the Spanish-speaking 6-year-old will, for example, have mastered much of the vocabulary and syntax of his or her oral language prior to coming to the United States. As these children learn English, they continue to be exposed to their native language at home, at school or in their community, developing additional skills in *both* languages. This process of dual language learning, however, may still adversely affect the child's academic performance in school.

According to Collier (1987, 1989), second-language learners who come to school between ages 8 and 12 may require anywhere from *5 to 7 years* to attain sufficient language proficiency to reach the 50th percentile on subject area tests of academic achievement in science, social studies, and reading. Yet, these children have had prior school experiences and increasingly complex cognitive and first-language development that can assist them to learn skills in their new language. In other words, the academic knowledge and concepts and the abstract language of classroom instruction learned in their first language can transfer and aid these children as they continue to learn science or other subjects while simultaneously learning English (Collier, 1995). The process, however, is obviously still a lengthy one.

On the other hand, those children who come to the United States and enter school from ages 5 to 7 haven't yet attained true fluency in their native language, nor have they had extended prior experiences with formal schooling and academic instruction (Collier, 1987, 1989). These children, for example, may not yet have learned important literacy skills such as reading and writing that can help them make a transfer to the second language. From *7 to 10 years* may be necessary for them to attain average performance in social studies, science, and reading when compared to native English speakers. Moreover, children coming to U.S. schools as adolescents frequently do not have enough time to learn their second language and achieve in academic content areas without a great deal of supportive instruction through the first language. Thus, Collier (1992) advocated continuing instruction in academic subjects through a student's first language while he or she is learning English.

In addition, Cummins (1982) argued that students learning a second language are at risk for identification as children with low intelligence, learning disabilities, or "deprived" home environments. That is, teachers may mistakenly assume that the child is language proficient because he or she demonstrates peer-appropriate everyday communications in social interactions with others. When the same child has difficulty with subject matter in the classroom, school professionals begin to seek a "within-child" or "within-the-home" explanation for his or her difficulty. Professionals may fail to recognize, however, that children learning a second language may attain Basic Interpersonal Communications Skills (BICS), skills useful in a social context, far faster than Cognitive-Academic Language Proficiency (CALP), those skills necessary to understand academic instruction (Cummins, 1996).

Although Cummins' work has been criticized, he has helped parents and school personnel to realize that *conversational* proficiency in English may not be sufficient for a complete understanding of *aca-*

demic discourse in the classroom. Subject areas have their own vocabulary, modes of thought, and abstract language of instruction. Thus, the child who can easily speak with friends on the playground might be confused in the classroom when his or her teacher says, "Susan has 13 koalas. John has 6 fewer koalas than Susan does. How many koalas does John have?" Similarly, most parents and teachers are proficient and literate speakers of the English language; however, they might find that listening to a lecture or reading a chapter on advanced nuclear physics will tax their level of comprehension. Thus, they might resort to feigning an interest in the topic or an understanding of the lecturer. So, too, Laura (see Chapter 1) inadvertently fooled the parents of her friends into believing that she was a native English speaker after only 1 year in the United States. Yet, as the academic instruction became increasingly more complex in her first- and second-grade classrooms, she began to fall behind and struggle compared to her U.S.-born friends. An inability to understand the academic language of instruction in the classroom places children such as Laura further and further at a disadvantage as they continually "lose out" on subject matter necessary for understanding the same topics at a deeper level in subsequent grades. Moreover, as children like Laura fall further behind their classmates in literacy skills such as reading, they read less than their peers and, therefore, learn less from reading and learn less about reading different types of texts than do their more proficient peers—a vicious cycle indeed!

Even more importantly, Gindis (2000) reminded parents and teachers that children of intercountry adoption, like Laura, can not properly be compared to children of immigrant parents. That is, rather than adding a second language to their first language as in the case of a bilingual child, children of intercountry adoption are instead losing their first language as they gain their new one. Children like Laura and my daughter, Katie, are first monolingual speakers of Russian or some other language and then later monolingual speakers of English. They are never really bilingual speakers at all. Moreover, most of these children will not have had sufficient opportunities to attend school or to become proficient in their first language before coming to the United States and most will have come from orphanage backgrounds having had only limited exposure to oral language in the first place.

On the other hand, according to Gindis (2000), children of intercountry adoptions coming to their new homes before the age of 4 will have a few years to catch up on language and concept skills before they enter school. Moreover, children arriving beyond the age of 8 may already have some skill in reading, writing, and speaking their native language that will transfer and assist them with their English language learning. Unfortunately, *children who come to the United States with their new parents between the ages of 4 and 8 are those who are most at risk. They haven't yet attained real proficiency in their first language, and they have little time to learn their new language prior to entering school.* These are the children who are often fluent in *conversational* English. Their apparent fluency in English, however, may cause parents and school personnel to believe that these children understand more subject matter information than they really do. Similarly, such seeming "ease" with English can also prompt parents and teachers to attribute any academic difficulty that might arise to the process of learning a new language and to overlook real language problems that may become increasingly hard to "fix" when the child grows older.

The long-term outcomes of language learning and school performance for children of intercountry adoption are, of course, still unknown. Some children will learn English quickly and catch up academically in school. Others will continue to struggle and fall farther behind peers as the gap widens between their facility with conversational English and their skill with academic language. Others will have true language delays and disorders requiring special education. Nevertheless, based on the work of Collier (1987, 1989), Cummins (1982, 1996), Gindis (2000), and Samway and McKeon (1999), we might make the following cautious generalizations regarding children of intercountry adoption as they acquire their new language:

- Poor pre- and postnatal health care, inadequate nutrition, low birth weight, infections, and exposure to environmental toxins before and after birth place these children at serious risk for language learning problems.
- An institutionalized background often precludes the normal development of the child's first language.
- Fluency with a first language facilitates learning a second language, but few children of intercountry adoption are truly fluent in their first language at the time of their adoption.
- Loss of the first language typically accompanies learning the new language; therefore, a child's language learning is disrupted and must begin anew.
- Ease in speaking a second language conversationally does not guarantee a child's later success in using the language to learn academic subjects in school.

- From 5 to 7 years or more may be necessary for children of intercountry adoption to attain language skills sufficient to profit from academic instruction delivered in English in U.S. classrooms; therefore, these children will need ongoing long-term academic support at school.

- Language disabilities requiring intervention may easily be overlooked by parents and school personnel who often attribute difficulty learning subject matter to the process of learning a second language.

✳ LANGUAGE DIFFERENCE OR DISABILITY?

School professionals are increasingly challenged to determine whether or not some children immigrating to the United States simply have a "language difference," speaking their native language as they attempt to learn English, or a language or learning disorder. That is, some children who are learning English may also have delays or disorders in learning or speaking their first language. Additionally, they may have some other type of physical, neurological, or cognitive disability that might prevent them from learning either language or academic subjects at an age-appropriate level.

Obviously, the mere fact that a 7-year-old child newly arrived in the United States is not yet understanding, speaking, reading, or writing English does not mean that the child has a language delay, a language disorder, or any other disability. This child is "language different" and is an English language learner. On the other hand, the 7-year-old child who comes to the United States without intelligible speech or without an ability to comprehend simple directions in his or her native language is likely to be language-delayed or language-disordered. Children with language disorders have difficulty understanding and expressing themselves age appropriately in their dominant language (e.g., they have unclear speech, cannot find the words to say what they want, use unusual word order, need much repetition of directions, or give inappropriate answers to questions). For children of intercountry adoption, who have limited experiences with language, with school-related topics, or with the processes of learning, differentiating between a language difference, a language disorder, or other disabilities requiring special education is even more difficult.

According to Ortiz and Garcia (1988) and Garcia and Ortiz (1988), however, teachers must take care not to refer children who are just learning English for an evaluation for special education placement without first taking several steps. For example, *teachers must consider not only whether or not the child is having academic difficulty, but also whether or not the instructional methods, curriculum, and expectations for learning are appropriate for the child.* When children are just learning English, these authorities recommend teachers consider the following questions:

- Is the child having difficulty learning and using conversational English correctly?
- Is the child having academic difficulty?
- Is the curriculum appropriate for the child? That is, has he or she had any prior experience with the topic under study (e.g., content knowledge or other skills such as asking questions, researching, or engaging in discussion about the topic)?
- Are the instructional materials and methods effective for language-minority students (e.g., involving children in collaborative learning arrangements, teaching content to mastery, embedding new materials to be learned in meaningful contexts)?
- Is the classroom environment conducive to learning and likely to enhance the child's motivation to learn (e.g., cultural sensitivity and appropriately challenging expectations on the part of the teacher)?
- Is the child having difficulty in more than one setting (e.g., with different teachers, at home, during interactions with friends)?
- Do the child's difficulties continue despite an appropriate curriculum and effective instructional methods?

Although these suggestions were designed for children of immigrant parents, they can also yield important diagnostic information for children of intercountry adoption. If the child is having academic and social difficulty in more than one setting despite an appropriate curriculum, classroom environment, and instruction, he or she may indeed have a language delay or a disorder in learning the words, structures, and functional uses of language. Or, the child might have some other disability affecting his or her performance in school. The parents and teachers may then agree to evaluate the child using standardized tests of language, academic, and cognitive skills in order to compare the child's performance to what is typical of same-age peers. Gindis (1998), however, cautions that school professionals should not compare the child's intellectual functioning to same-age peers in the United States. Professionals must realize that these children are unique—they simply will not have the knowledge base and skills of their classmates and the ease with which they learn English will not necessarily be a direct indicator of their overall cognitive ability.

Parents and school professionals must also remember that commercially prepared standardized instruments to evaluate reading, writing, and other language or cognitive skills may or may not be available in the student's native language. Several tests of basic skills are available for administration in Spanish and some tests have versions translated to Chinese, Korean, Vietnamese, and so forth, although few tests are readily available translated to Russian. Nevertheless, the results of these tests must be carefully interpreted because English language learners usually are not part of the population on which these tests were standardized, and words and concepts contained on these tests may not translate exactly from English to the child's native language. Moreover, children of intercountry adoption are still adjusting to significant changes in their lives that can lower their test performance. Additionally, they most likely have limited or no experience with formal schooling, with test-taking, or with the concepts often contained on these tests, making interpretation of their scores on standardized tests difficult or even meaningless.

Because standardized tests are inherently biased, larger school districts with greater numbers of English language learners often administer a dual-language assessment, particularly when eligibility for special education is under consideration. A dual-language assessment can determine the child's proficiency and skills with his or her native language, establish the child's level of proficiency in English, and identify the child's dominant language, if any. That is, the child may be tested in his or her native language only, in English only, or in both languages depending on the child's length of time in the United States and his or her age, cognitive ability, and apparent proficiency with English. For example, sometimes the child might be tested in English but retested in the native language on items on which he or she makes an error. Furthermore, correct responses in either language can be accepted to reduce the language and cultural bias of standardized tests.

Providing even more information than formal standardized testing to determine whether or not children just learning to speak English have a language delay or disorder or some other type of disability, however, is the child's actual performance when given tasks to complete at home or in the classroom. Garcia and Ortiz (1988) and Gindis (1998) advocated a pretest, teach, retest, reteach approach for children having limited English and less experience with formalized learning. Such an approach may be particularly appropriate for children of intercountry adoption. That is, school professionals might present a young child with common objects and ask the child in either the first language and/or English to "Show me the pencil." If the child is unable to do this, the professional can quickly prompt the child by pointing and saying, "This is the pencil. Show me the pencil." Similarly, the teacher can ask the child to find a red crayon or place three plastic number counters on the table. Observing the speed at which children are able to respond to such tasks after being given any necessary assistance can yield valuable information regarding their ability to learn language and concepts.

According to Gindis (1998), parents and school professionals having a school-aged child of intercountry adoption are wise *not* to take a "wait-and-see" attitude regarding the child's readiness for learning language and academics. That is, he suggested evaluating the child quickly within the first 2 to 8 weeks of his or her arrival in the United States. At this time, a bilingual speech-language professional can conduct an evaluation in the native language in order to determine the child's first language proficiency, and his or her cognitive abilities can be assessed by a bilingual psychologist through nonverbal measures. Such an evaluation, although difficult to obtain in many areas of the country, may enable parents and teachers to determine whether or not the child requires special education assistance and help beyond that typical of most English language learners.

For example, some children of intercountry adoption have hearing impairments that may have delayed acquisition of their first language and that may affect their second-language acquisition (Groze & Ileana, 1996; Miller & Hendrie, 2000). Such hearing impairments may even be the result of ear infections incurred as formula drains into the eustachian tubes during "bottle propping," a routine practice for feeding infants in some orphanages. Obviously, a thorough evaluation of the child's hearing is imperative soon on arrival home. Other children of intercountry adoption have alcohol-related birth defects or physical conditions such as a cleft palate affecting their ability to learn or to speak the language (Ryan, 2000).

Still others have central auditory processing disorders. These children possess adequate hearing; however, they are unable to interpret and make sense out of what they hear. Children with central auditory processing difficulty may have trouble paying attention to what others are saying or they may have a hard time remembering and sequencing information they hear. Given a series of oral directions, for example, the child may remember to "go to the bookshelf," but he or she may not remember to "get the big red book and bring it back over here." Similarly, the child may be unable to ignore the squeak of a nearby chair or the hum of an overhead light in order to attend to what the teacher is saying. Other children with central auditory processing problems may have difficulty detecting the difference between similar sounding words such as "think" and "thing" or "pig" and "peg," and many others have trouble answering questions or making appropriate contributions to conversations. Frequently asking for information to be repeated or confusion, restlessness, and inattention during auditory activities may signal difficulty with central auditory processing. Of course, these same behaviors can be seen in children with ADHD or children who are frustrated or simply bored as well.

Obviously, the ability to pay attention to information received through auditory means is essential as children go up the grades at school. Following oral directions, listening to the teacher's instructions, remembering and sequencing the events in a story as the teacher reads aloud, participating in classroom discussions, and maintaining attention are key skills for all students. Moreover, the ability to detect and produce rhyming words, to detect separate words within sentences, to discriminate separate sounds or parts within words, and to segment, blend, or delete words parts are important auditory skills prerequisite for later learning to read. Essential phonological awareness, or phonemic awareness, skills as these are often lacking in children later diagnosed with learning disabilities who have difficulty reading (Adams, 1990; Snow, Burns, & Griffin, 1998).

English (2000) and Kranowitz (1998) offered a number of suggestions for teachers to help children having central auditory processing problems. These include the following:

- Seat the child away from sources of noise such as open windows, doorways, or air conditioners.
- Allow the child to use headphones during independent work requiring concentration.
- Have the child repeat back directions or information to be remembered.
- Provide written or other visual cues (e.g., sequenced pictures for directions, lists, written notes, etc.).
- Teach vocabulary or important concepts prior to their use in classroom activities.

- Use simple language.
- Break directions or tasks into shorter steps.

Certainly, not all children of intercountry adoption will have difficulty with central auditory processing. Moreover, detecting the difference between a child having a central auditory processing problem and one simply learning to speak English is a task for trained speech-language professionals. For those children suspected of having central auditory processing disorders, however, remedial special education services may be provided (see Chapter 6).

Unfortunately, in many states non-English-speaking students without obvious disabilities (e.g., visual or hearing impairments or autism) are routinely excluded from special education programs for a period of time, such as 1 year, while they receive initial services for children having English as a second language. The Individuals with Disabilities Education Act (IDEA, 1997), however, specifically extends special education services to these students, although it prevents their placement in such programs solely on the basis of their limited proficiency with English. Nevertheless, careful assessment as quickly as possible on a child's arrival in the United States may help to determine a child's potential for learning. Such an assessment also may prove a child eligible for special education who may otherwise have gone unnoticed, thus wasting valuable time necessary to optimize his or her language skills and academic performance.

Fortunately, public schools today offer assistance for students having language delays or difficulty learning language skills due to neurological, physical, or cognitive disabilities including central auditory processing disorders. Such assistance is available through special education programs mandated at both the federal and state level (see Chapter 6). In addition, for the many children new to the United States who simply need to learn English as a second language many schools now provide special assistance for them and for their teachers.

❈ SCHOOL SERVICES FOR ESL

Proficiency understanding and speaking the English language is, of course, essential for successful learning in U.S. classrooms. Schools typically refer to students for whom English is a second language as ESL students, as English for Speakers of Other Languages (ESOL) students, or as Limited English Proficiency (LEP) students. In this chapter, however, I refer to students less than proficient in English as *English language learners* (ELL) because this term includes not only those just learning English but also students possessing sufficient conversational English yet lacking adequate skills to comprehend fully the abstract language of academic instruction (Rivera, 1994).

Federal legislation passed in 1994, Public Law 103-382 (the Improving America's Schools Act) states that students shall not be admitted to or excluded from federally assisted education programs merely on the basis of a surname or language-minority status. Thus, federal grants are available to help states and schools provide ELLs with equal opportunities to achieve the same standards set forth for all students in the state and/or school. Furthermore, the Improving America's Schools Act defines the LEP student as one who:

A.

    1. was not born in the United States or whose native language is a language other than English and comes from an environment where a language other than English is dominant; or,

    2. is a Native American or Alaska Native who is a native resident of the outlying areas and comes from an environment where a language other than English has had a significant impact on such individual's level of English language proficiency; or,

    3. is migratory and whose native language is other than English and comes from an environment where a language other than English is dominant; and

B. has sufficient difficulty speaking, reading, writing, or understanding the English language and whose difficulties may deny such individual the opportunity to learn successfully in classrooms where the language of instruction is English or to participate fully in our society. (IASA, Title VII, Part E, Section 7501)

The federal legislation does not mandate particular types of programs, but it does provide incentives for a range of services to meet the unique needs of individual states, school districts, and schools. Obviously, some states and schools will have larger populations of ELL students and thus may have more well-developed services than states or schools with fewer such students. In fact, the quantity and quality of programs for ELL students varies greatly across the country with school divisions in large metropolitan areas frequently having more ELL students and a greater range of services available in multiple languages than those in rural areas. Nevertheless, "typical" services for ELL students often include the following:

- Special "self-contained" classrooms in which students from diverse languages are taught as a group, receiving *intensive* instruction in English prior to placement in a regular classroom
- "Pull-out programs" in which students of various native languages receive intensive instruction in English language skills in a separate classroom and return to a regular classroom throughout the day for integration in other activities with age-appropriate peers
- "Collaborative programs" in which ELL students remain in the regular classroom with same-age peers with instruction in English embedded in the context of ongoing academic activities and assistance provided to the teacher in modifying or adapting instruction as needed.

Sometimes schools offer "bilingual" education programs, although the law does not require these services to be provided. In bilingual education programs, instruction occurs in *both* the child's languages. That is, the child may receive instruction in the English language and continued development of skills in his or her native language. Additionally, the child usually receives academic subject matter instruction in his or her native language, or in English supplemented with the native language, as necessary for all or any part of the school curriculum. Study of the history and culture associated with the student's native language is also usually considered an important part of bilingual education.

Interestingly, some authorities recommend bilingual education for children of intercountry adoption (Melina, 1998), whereas others (Gindis, 2000) do not. Melina, for example, asserted that older children must be permitted to use their native language as long as it is helpful to them. She argued that bilingual education increases the opportunity for these children to use and analyze language and to explore new concepts. According to Melina (1998), although these children may eventually lose their first language, the intellectual challenge of language learning results in enhanced educational achievement.

Unfortunately, however, most children of intercountry adoption do not have a well-established first language. Gindis (2000), therefore, did not recommend bilingual education for children of intercountry adoption unless their parents are truly bilingual, continue to speak the first language at home, and interact frequently with other native language speakers in the community. The vast majority of children of intercountry adoption will come to monolingual English-speaking homes in which the first language will not be supported and ultimately will be lost. Gindis (2000) suggested that a short-term or "transitional" bilingual education program may be appropriate for some older children of intercountry adoption who have attained a degree of proficiency in their language. On the other hand, he maintained that long-term attempts through bilingual education to preserve the child's first language, which is most likely rather limited in the first place, may result in confusion and delay the process of learning the language necessary for adjustment—English. Avoiding bilingual education programs, however, does not preclude the child's identification and eligibility for assistance as an ELL through the other types of services previously described.

Frequently, the process of identifying ELL students begins with the school administering a "home language" survey whenever students register in the school division. If on this survey parents indicate that there is a language other than or in addition to English spoken in the home, the school may initiate an assessment of the child's English language proficiency. Students of intercountry adoption certainly meet the first and second criteria for the federal definition of LEP. That is, they were not born in the United States, their native language and original language environment were not English, and they may have sufficient difficulty with English to prevent their success in classrooms where English is dominant. As a matter of fact, Gindis (2000) asserted that school-aged children of intercountry adoption are almost certainly eligible for ESL services in their school. Children of intercountry adoption, however, are likely to *come from homes speaking only English*. Therefore, the home-language survey may not properly identify these children nor will they match the pattern "typical" of most immigrant ESL students. Parents and teachers must take the initiative to inform the school and serve as advocates when children require assessment or identification for services as an ELL.

Although federal legislation does not mandate any specific method for identifying students as ELL, all school districts are required to develop a system for receiving and evaluating these students. In larger school divisions, a formal center may exist with personnel skilled in conducting bilingual interviews and administering various tests in many different languages. In smaller school systems, however, a principal, assistant principal, guidance counselor, speech-language therapist, school psychologist, or some other professional may assume this responsibility, with or without the help of an interpreter. Regardless of the actual process used, the assessment must include multiple criteria and not just a single test with the focus of the assessment on native language skills, proficiency in understanding and speaking English, and evaluation of reading, writing, or other content area skills in English as appropriate. Moreover, the IDEA (1997) requires non-discriminatory evaluation using multiple criteria and bilingual assessment whenever students having English as a second language are being considered for special education services (see Chapter 6).

Regardless of the way in which children are identified and served in programs for English language learners, teachers and other school personnel can do much to assist these children within the classroom. Sensitivity to the needs of ELL students, whether or not they are formally identified for service as ESL or LEP students, can help these youngsters experience greater success alongside their peers.

※ CLASSROOM APPROACHES FOR ENGLISH LANGUAGE LEARNERS

Helping older children of intercountry adoption learn and practice their new English skills is an exciting task for both parents and teachers! Fortunately, much of what parents and school personnel can do to assist these children to learn the English language is simple and sensible. Although some parents and schools use the services of translators, "commonsense," practical strategies include pictures, cue cards, pantomime, "peer buddies," language expansion, and music.

A peer buddy assigned by the teacher, for example, can assist the child with limited English skills to complete class work or to navigate the school building. Daily routines and task directions at home or at school can be sketched using simple picture clues and placed in sequence on index cards on a flip-ring or in a photo album. Alternatively, teachers can take photographs with a digital camera of children in the classroom completing daily activities and place these in a series for viewing by the child (or other children requiring additional assistance) whenever needed. Similarly, stories or math problems can be "acted out" by students in the class or illustrated through picture sequences to enhance understanding for everyone, including the ELL student.

Moreover, as ELLs begin to speak and participate in class, parents and teachers must take care not to correct their language errors, but rather to model and expand the correct language forms. For example, if 9-year-old Laura says, "The girl *hitted* the ball" (a common over-generalization for many young children who learn English as their first language), the parent or teacher might respond with "Yes, the girl *hit* the ball and then she ran very fast to first base." Such an approach provides correction without calling attention to the error and also offers the child a model of a more complex grammatical structure. In addition, language expansion and constantly "talking aloud" about what you or the child are doing helps the child label actions and learn additional concepts such as number, color, texture, or relative position in space. Parents, for example, have long given "commentary" while they work or while young children play such as, "I can stack the groceries on top of the table," or "You have a red block, a green block, and a blue block. You have three blocks," or "Wow, you are filling the bucket up with sand. I bet the sand feels rough and hot." Although parents give commentary naturally with infants and toddlers, they often forget to do so with the older child learning to speak English. Yet, talking naturally and consistently about ongoing activities affords many wonderful opportunities for children of all ages to expand vocabulary and increase listening and other language skills.

Teachers might also consider instructing aides and classroom volunteers in the use of commentary and appropriate ways to correct errors. When these assistants are providing instruction to children, they have a legitimate need to know that the child has an accent or that he or she is just learning English. This knowledge is particularly important during classroom assessments. My daughter, Katie, for example, once read a list of sight words to a parent volunteer who was to "check off" the words Katie could read. Katie pronounced the word "pretty" as "pity" and became quite upset when the parent volunteer would not accept her insistence that she knew the word. She simply could not yet say it properly due to her accent! Her inability to pronounce the word correctly was no different, however, than an African-American child who says "mo" instead of "more." When teachers know children are ELL, they must remember to explain this to instructional assistants and conduct sensitive evaluations of performance themselves.

Parent or teacher commentary regarding daily, ongoing activities increases exposure to the English language, and so, too, does music. Parents of children of intercountry adoption often say that their children respond early and eagerly to music. Katie, for example, learned a great deal of language by watching *Barney* and his friends sing songs on videotapes over and over again and by singing simple songs like "Twinkle Twinkle Little Star" with her parents during short car trips to the store. Similarly, teachers can permit ELL students to listen to music on headphones or to read along with illustrated stories on tape. Poems, rhymes, rhythmic chants, games, and songs all can help develop vocabulary and essential oral language skills like the sound and rhythm of English for these children.

Many practical suggestions to help teachers improve the classroom performance of students of intercountry adoption who are just learning the English language can be found on line in handbooks for ESL programs at department of education Web sites for the states. Other suggestions for teachers, and with a few modifications for parents as well, include the following:

- Listen to children in their attempts to communicate. Allow children to say what they can rather than finishing for them or correcting their speech and grammar. Respond to what children have to say rather than to how they say it.

- Seat the student close to the front of the room or close to activities. Permit the student and his or her peer buddy to move about the classroom as necessary.

- Speak to the student using a normal rate of speech rather than a slower speed. Use complete sentences but simplify your vocabulary initially. Write key vocabulary or direction words on the board as you use them, and use picture clues and concrete objects to illustrate major concepts. Also, make use of media such as videotapes and interactive computer software when appropriate.

- Show students how to do things rather than relying on verbal directions and "lecture." If this is not always possible, have an instructional assistant, a parent volunteer, a resource teacher in ESL, or a peer buddy review key vocabulary, information, and concepts *before* they are needed in the classroom activity. Structuring activities and information in advance will help students of intercountry adoption feel more confident in their ability to understand and participate.

- Realize that children will develop listening ability in their new language before they achieve fluency in speaking. They may remain silent in class for a period of time. Listening intently is exhausting; therefore, teachers might permit ELL students to "take a break" from classroom activities periodically. Additionally, remember that these "silent children" may not speak up and ask a question even when they do not understand the activities or directions. As a matter of fact, some children may actually nod or smile as if they do understand when they really do not. Teachers are advised to approach children with limited English skills and privately assist them. Answer their questions, ask them specific questions to check their understanding, and have them explain to you or show you what they are to do.

- Consider placing the child of intercountry adoption who "catches on quickly" in an average or higher reading group. Permitting the child to be a listening member of such a group provides him or her with models of good language usage.

- Provide the child with high interest–low reading level materials. Age-appropriate stories and textbooks covering grade-level content are available at lower reading levels to help the child learn information while still a "beginning" reader. Reading teachers or teachers of students with learning disabilities frequently have access to various high interest–low reading level materials. For older students who are already reading in their first language, seek assistance from the school library-media specialist or ESL teacher to obtain relevant materials in the child's native language.

- Label objects in the classroom in English and in the child's first language if possible and consider enlisting the help of a volunteer or translator to teach the other children in the classroom some basic vocabulary in the child's native language.

- Read aloud to children daily.

- Use language-learning programs and approaches such as Bright Start (Haywood, 1992) or Fast ForWord (Merzenich et al., 1996; Tallal et al., 1996). Although any one "program" or "approach" must always be used cautiously, Bright Start is a systematic program that builds essential language concepts for preschoolers in seven areas including self-regulation, numbers, comparisons, perspective-taking, classifying, sequencing and patterns, and letters and shapes. In addition, Fast ForWord utilizes computer technology to build phonological awareness skills (e.g., detecting differences in similar sounds such as "cat" and "cap"), critical for later success in reading. Central auditory processing, memory, and grammar are additional skills featured in this computer-game format.

- Initially, ask factual, simple questions regarding classroom activities that you know the student can answer such as, "What happened when the magnet touched the steel?" or "What happened when it touched the paper?" Later, expand to more open-ended questions like "What do magnets do?"

- Provide additional time for ELL students to complete assignments, perhaps breaking them into smaller increments for these students.

- Allow alternative response formats for all students whenever possible. For example, rather than requiring a written response, permit students to illustrate their knowledge using pictures, a graphic organizer, or some other nonverbal means. Similarly, allow students to take tests privately using an appropriate response mode (e.g., oral testing, hands-on demonstration of knowledge, simple fill-in the blank with a word bank, or simple multiple-choice questions). Whenever possible, refrain from penalizing students for spelling or grammatical errors in written work when *content knowledge* and not writing skills are being assessed.

- Respect cultural or "institutionally induced" differences such as need for personal space, making eye contact, and asking questions (e.g., making eye contact or asking questions of someone in authority may be viewed as disrespect by some children of intercountry adoption).

- Provide realistic, culturally sensitive reading materials and integrate information and language from the child's birth country into lessons whenever applicable as a bridge or scaffold for new learning.

- Realize that students may lack vocabulary and concepts and that some words may not adequately translate from the child's first language to English. Never assume the child understands, but rather define and illustrate common American terms such as "astronaut," "candy cane," or "football."

- Hold appropriate and challenging high expectations for children of intercountry adoption and provide positive feedback frequently.

❊ CONCLUSION

Language delays are often noted in the medical histories of children adopted from orphanages abroad. Many children will overcome these initial delays, learn English, and achieve alongside their classmates at school. Others will have significant language disabilities or more subtle language-learning problems related to early institutionalization that will affect school performance. The long-term impact of language learning on the academic achievement of children of intercountry adoption, however, is only now beginning to be investigated.

Assuming no physical or neurological difficulties are interfering with normal development, children who are adopted internationally as infants will most likely learn to speak English much like American-born children do. Those who are adopted after the age of 8 may have attained proficiency in their native language and gained experiences with schooling that may transfer and assist them in learning English. These children may also benefit from ESL services and, perhaps, from bilingual education, in their schools.

On the other hand, children who are adopted between the ages of 4 and 8, particularly those who arrive from institutionalized environments, are at high risk for language-learning problems at school. These children have most likely suffered language deprivation during lengthy stays in an orphanage and they have not yet attained real fluency in their first language. Interestingly, these children often lose their native language rapidly and appear to learn English with ease. Conversational English in social settings, however, develops much faster than does the abstract and complex language of instruction in the classroom. These children may take from 7 to 10 years to attain the degree of language proficiency necessary to perform academically at the same level as their chronological-age peers—*at least half of their overall time spent in the American school system!*

Moreover, language-learning difficulties for these children are often "overlooked" by parents and teachers because these children seem so verbal and fluent in daily conversations. Professionals, for example, may take a "wait and see" approach, failing to diagnose actual language disabilities because they believe these children's difficulties are due simply to the process of learning a new language and adjusting to a new culture. Unfortunately, as these children advance up the grades, language deficits, resulting in concomitant losses in learning and achievement, may send some into a downward spiral of frustration and failure.

Children of intercountry adoption should have an immediate and thorough evaluation of hearing and of language development in their native tongue, particularly those who enter after the age of 3. As these children enter the preschool or kindergarten, they may not fit the "typical" pattern of children eligible for ESL, nevertheless, many of them will benefit from these services. Evaluation by a trained speech and language professional, along with careful observation by parents and school personnel of the speed with which the child learns language, new concepts and skills, may help to differentiate between those children having language or other disabilities and those who are simply English language learners.

Chapter 6

Accessing Special Education and Section 504 Services

C hildren of intercountry adoption who come to the United States as infants may grow and develop just the same as do other children born to U.S. citizens. Many other children of intercountry adoption will catch up with their chronological-age peers once they arrive home and adjust to their new surroundings, family, and language. Those arriving at ages 5 and above may certainly receive help learning the English language once they enter the schools through ESL or LEP programs such as those described in Chapter 5.

Of particular interest, however, are studies of children of intercountry adoption who have been with their parents from 1 to 4 years. Between 15% and 25% of children adopted from institutions in Romania, Russia, and the former Soviet States require special education for speech and language delays, developmental delays, learning disabilities, or emotional/behavioral disorders during their preschool or school years (Groze & Ileana, 1996; McGuiness, 2000). Thus, the percentage of children of intercountry adoption who are receiving some form of special education is considerably larger than what would be expected given that not quite 12% of the overall school-age population is placed in such programs (U.S. Department of Education,

2000). Although schools often do not know how to test, teach, and respond to the needs of children coming from institutions abroad, federal legislation does exist to ensure that students with disabilities are given a free, appropriate public education (Schell-Frank, 2000).

❋ SPECIAL EDUCATION

The Individuals with Disabilities Education Act Amendment of 1997 (IDEA, 1997) guarantees that all children with disabilities are to receive a free and appropriate public education. This means that no child can be refused an education by the schools regardless of the severity of that child's disability. This also means that each child with a disability is guaranteed special education and related services to meet his or her unique needs and to prepare him or her for employment and independent living.

According to IDEA (1997), a child with a disability is a child with mental retardation, hearing impairments, speech or language impairments, visual impairments, serious emotional disturbance, orthopedic impairments, autism, traumatic brain injury, other health impairments or specific learning disabilities who needs special education and related services. For children age birth through 9, disability can also mean, at the discretion of the state, a developmental delay that requires early intervention or specific preschool programming (see Table 6.1). Special education is defined as specially designed instruction to meet the unique needs of a child with a disability including instruction in the classroom, in the home, in hospitals and institutions, and in other settings. Related services are those services required to assist a child with a disability to benefit from the special education to be provided. These include special transportation, speech-language pathology and audiology services, psychological services, physical and occupational therapy, therapeutic recreation, social work services, counseling services, orientation and mobility services, and diagnostic and evaluation services for the early identification and assessment of disabilities in children.

In order to receive the benefits of special education and related services, children must first be determined eligible. That is, they must be identified as "children with disabilities" according to IDEA and to the regulations of the state in which they reside. The definitions of disability, criteria for eligibility, age restrictions, and processes vary somewhat from state to state and, to some degree, from school district to school district. Parents and school professionals, therefore,

Table 6.1
Disabilities Covered under IDEA, 1997

Categorical	Common Definition
Autism	A developmental disability significantly affecting verbal and nonverbal communication and social interaction, generally evident before age 3, that adversely affects a child's educational performance. Other characteristics often associated with autism are engagement in repetitive activities and stereotyped movements, resistance to environmental change or daily routines, and unusual responses to sensory experiences.
Developmental Delay	*For infants and toddlers under age 3:* As measured by appropriate diagnostic instruments and procedures...a child experiencing delay in one or more of the areas of development: cognitive, physical, communication, social/emotional, or adaptive; or has a diagnosed physical or mental condition which has a high probability of resulting in developmental delay; and may also include, at a state's discretion, at-risk infants and toddlers. *For children aged 3 through 9:* As defined by the state and as measured by appropriate diagnostic instruments and procedures...a child experiencing delay in one or more of the following areas of development: physical, cognitive, communication, social/emotional, or adaptive; and who by reason thereof, needs special education and related services.
Hearing Impairment	Children with hearing impairments, including deafness, that are so severe as to impair the child's processing of linguistic information through hearing, with or without amplification, that adversely affects educational performance.
Mental Retardation	Characterized by significantly sub-average intellectual functioning, existing concurrently with related limitations in two or more applicable adaptive skills areas (communication, self-care, home living, social skills, community use, self-direction, health/safety, functional academics, leisure, and work). Manifests before age 18.
Orthopedic Impairment	Includes an impairment caused by a congenital anomaly (e.g., clubfoot, absence of some member, etc.), an impairment caused by disease (e.g., poliomyelitis, bone tuberculosis, etc.), and an impairment from any other cause (e.g., cerebral palsy, amputations, and fractures or burns which cause contractures). [States typically add "which adversely affects educational performance."]
Other Health Impaired	Means having limited strength, vitality, or alertness, due to chronic or acute health problems such as heart condition, tuberculosis, rheumatic fever, nephritis, asthma, sickle cell anemia, hemophilia, epilepsy, lead poisoning, leukemia, or diabetes. [States typically add "which adversely affects educational performance."]
Serious Emotional Disturbance	Means a condition exhibiting one or more of the following characteristics over a long period of time and to a marked degree, which adversely affects educational performance: a.) An inability to learn which cannot be explained by intellectual, sensory, and health factors; b.) An inability to build or maintain satisfactory interpersonal relationships with peers and teachers; c.) Inappropriate types of behavior or feelings under normal circumstances; d.) A general pervasive mood of unhappiness or depression; or e.) A tendency to develop physical symptoms or fears associated with personal or school problems. The term includes children who are schizophrenic. The term does not include children who are socially maladjusted, unless it is determined that they are emotionally disturbed.

Table 6.1 continued

Specific Learning Disability	A disorder in one or more of the basic psychological processes involved in understanding or using language spoken or written, which may manifest itself in an imperfect ability to listen, think, read, write, spell, or to do mathematical calculations. The term includes such conditions as perceptual handicaps, brain injury, minimal brain dysfunction, and developmental aphasia. The term does not include learning problems which are primarily the result of visual, hearing, or motor handicaps, of mental retardation, of emotional disturbance, or of environmental, cultural, or economic disadvantage.
Speech and Language Impairment	A communication disorder, such as stuttering, impaired articulation, a language impairment, or a voice impairment, which adversely affects a child's educational performance. [This diagnosis, however, cannot be made solely on the basis of limited English proficiency.]
Traumatic Brain Injury	An acquired injury to the brain caused by an external physical force, resulting in total or partial functional disability or psychosocial impairment, or both, that adversely affects a child's educational performance. The term applies to open or closed head injuries resulting in impairments in one or more areas such as cognition; language; memory; attention; reasoning; abstract thinking; judgment; problem-solving; sensory, perceptual and motor ability; psychosocial behavior physical functions; information processing and speech. The term does not apply to brain injuries that are congenital or degenerative, or brain injuries induced by birth trauma.
Visual Impairment	An impairment in vision that, even with correction, adversely affects a child's educational performance. The term includes both partial sight and blindness.

must consult their own state department of education for specific information relative to where they live. Nevertheless, the essential elements of the process guaranteed under IDEA (1997) include child find; multidisciplinary and nondiscriminatory assessment; parent consultation; due process; the Individualized Education Program (IEP); placement in the least restrictive environment (LRE); provisions for early intervention for preschoolers; and infants and toddlers with disabilities.

Child Find

Under IDEA (1997), states and school districts must make every possible effort to identify and serve all children with disabilities who need special education assistance. The child find provision, then, requires school districts to "advertise" that free services are available. School systems, for example, might conduct public awareness campaigns or periodically offer free "child checks" to detect delays in cognitive, motor, language, or social skills in preschoolers. Additionally, elementary schools might routinely "screen" kindergartners, first graders, or new students in areas such as hearing, vision, speech, or language skills to determine whether or not additional evaluation is needed. Too, parents, teachers, doctors, day-care workers, or any other individual may make a referral to initiate the process of formal evaluation to determine a child's eligibility for special education.

Evaluation, however, can be a relatively lengthy process and the determination that a child has a "disability" is certainly a serious matter. Therefore, unless a child has an obvious disability, states usually require parents, teachers, and other school professionals to work together to document how they have attempted to meet the needs of that child within the regular classroom *before* they make a referral for special education evaluation. Teacher assistance teams (Chalfant, Pysh, & Moultrie, 1979), prereferral intervention teams (Safran & Safran, 1996), or child study teams, made up of teachers, counselors, psychologists, and others, often work together to create change in the classroom environment, curriculum, or instruction when children are having academic or behavioral difficulty. Moving a child's seat to a less distracting location, providing positive rewards for completing work, or posting an outline of the day's lesson on an overhead projector, for example, are simple changes that can make the difference between success and failure. When parents and professionals make good faith attempts to help children but do not observe the expected progress, they can be confident that they are not making frivolous referrals. They will also have additional documentation regarding how the child learns and how well the child responds to particular interventions that can be extremely useful during the formal evaluation process.

Multidisciplinary and Nondiscriminatory Assessment

Multidisciplinary and nondiscriminatory assessment are IDEA (1997) requirements that children must be evaluated in all areas of suspected disability and in a manner that is not biased by culture, language, or disability. This means that a team of qualified professionals must participate in the decision-making process and that information must be gathered in relevant areas, as necessary, including the child's health, vision, hearing, social and emotional status, general intelligence, academic performance, motor abilities, and speech and language skills.

Typical formal assessments include gathering educational, medical, sociocultural, psychological, and developmental data. No single test or test score can be the sole criterion for placement in special education and the evaluation must provide information to assist the team in determining the educational needs of the child. Moreover, under IDEA each test administered must be technically sound; validated for the specific purpose for which it is being used; selected and administered so as not to be discriminatory on a racial or cultural basis; given by trained, qualified professionals; and selected and given in the child's native language or mode of communication unless it is clearly not feasible to do so.

The child's eligibility for special education also must be reevaluated at least every 3 years. This "triennial review" can involve, if necessary, the same extensive and formal assessments required for the initial placement in special education. However, IDEA (1997) streamlines the process of triennial evaluation by permitting a team of teachers, parents, and other professionals (i.e., the IEP team) to determine what, if any, information needs to be gathered in order to make an informed decision regarding the child's continuing special education eligibility.

Parent Consultation and Right to Due Process

No one individual can unilaterally place a child in special education or remove the child from his or her placement. Parents and schools, therefore, both possess certain procedural rights under IDEA (1997). For example, before the child can be formally evaluated to determine his or her eligibility for special education, the parent must be informed and give consent. That is, parents must be told in their native language and in a manner they can understand the specific types of tests that may be given and the purpose for which the information gathered might be used (i.e., possible placement in special education). In addition, the parent has a right to see and receive copies of his or her child's records, including copies of the test reports and justification for any decisions made. The parent also has the right to expect that these records will be kept confidential and that the school must consider any information or documentation he or she might present.

Additionally, parents have the right to be informed and to give their consent before their child is placed in or removed from any special education program. Moreover, they have the right to disagree with the school system at any time. If parents, for example, do not want their child placed in a special education program or removed from an existing placement, they have the right to refuse and to have their child "stay put" in his or her current classroom until the disagreement is resolved. IDEA (1997) and state regulations specify a multilevel process to resolve disputes including mediation, local and state hearings, and even court appeals.

Other procedural safeguards under IDEA (1997) include independent evaluations and recovery of legal expenses. Schools, for example, must pay for legal fees when court hearings result in decisions favorable to the parents. So, too, parents may disagree with the results of the school's evaluation or with the school's refusal to administer tests the parents deem appropriate. Thus, parents may seek an independent evaluation by a qualified psychologist or other professional not employed by the school district. Because the typical standardized tests given by schools to determine eligibility for special education may be inappropriate for children of intercountry adoption, parents may find an independent evaluation to be particularly helpful. School personnel must consider data from this independent evaluation, and if the results support the parents' views, the school district can be held responsible for paying the cost of the evaluation.

Furthermore, rights to due process extend to disciplinary actions regarding children with disabilities (IDEA, 1997). The child with a disability who also has behavioral problems must have in place a behavior intervention plan that is based on a careful analysis of the factors controlling his or her behavior (i.e., a Functional Behavior Assessment) and that is reasonably calculated to promote positive behavior change. Thus, if a child makes inappropriate comments or gestures in the classroom, teachers and other school professionals must observe carefully and collect data to determine the context of the child's actions. Perhaps, for example, the child only engages in the misbehavior during math time, an area of difficulty and frustration for him or her. Or similarly, perhaps the data indicates that other children in the classroom laugh and pay attention to the child following the inappropriate comments and gestures and that this attention is controlling and continuing the misbehavior. Recommendations for changing the methods of instruction or classroom management used during math time, then, can be included in the behavior intervention plan and the results of these changes monitored and documented.

When children with disabilities misbehave, however, they may receive short-term suspensions, consistent with state regulations, for up to 10 days for their misbehavior. Before children with disabilities can be suspended for a period of time longer than 10 days or before they can be expelled, however, the school division must first ensure that an appropriate behavior intervention plan was in place. If not, the school must conduct a functional behavior assessment and construct the behavior intervention plan. If, on the other hand, an appropriate behavior intervention plan did exist, the school must first conduct a Manifestation Determination Review before suspending or expelling the child.

The purpose of the Manifestation Determination Review is to determine whether or not the child's misbehavior is related to or caused by his or her disability. A team of individuals must decide, for example, whether or not the child has the cognitive ability to understand the consequences of his or her actions or the ability to control those actions. If the team determines that the misbehavior was a manifestation of the disability, then the child cannot be suspended or expelled. Rather, the team must reconsider the child's behavior intervention plan, special education, and related services that are being received. If the team decides that the misbehavior and disability were unrelated, then normal disciplinary procedures can be followed. When a child breaks the law, however, the school may of course notify juvenile authorities. And finally, when a child's behavior is highly dangerous or disruptive, or if the child possesses a weapon or illegal substances on school property, he or she can be removed for up to 45 days to an approved interim alternative school while the manifestation determination review takes place (Yell, 1998).

The Individualized Education Program

Before a child can be placed in a special education program, a document called the IEP must be constructed. The IEP is developed by a team including, at a minimum, the special educator, the regular classroom teacher, the parent(s), a school administrator or his or her designee, and the child him or herself whenever appropriate. The IEP can be no older than one calendar year and can be renegotiated at any time at the request of any of the IEP team members, including the parents or the teacher(s). Although no one standard IEP form exists, according to IDEA (1997) the IEP must contain, among other things, the following information:

- A statement of the child's present levels of educational performance, including how the child's disability affects his or her involvement and progress in the general curriculum (or for preschool children in appropriate activities)

- A statement of measurable annual goals, including benchmarks or short-term objectives to meet the child's needs and enable the child to be involved in and progress in the general curriculum

- A statement regarding how the child's progress toward the annual goals will be measured and how the parents will be regularly informed at least as often as parents of children without disabilities of their child's progress toward the goals and the extent to which that progress is sufficient to help the child meet the goals by the end of the year

- A statement of the special education and related services and supplementary aids and services to be provided to the child, and a statement of the program modifications or supports for school personnel that will be provided for the child to advance toward attaining the annual goals, be involved in and progress in the general curriculum, and be educated and participate with children with and without disabilities

- An explanation of the extent, if any, to which the child will not participate with nondisabled children in the regular class

- A statement of any individual modifications in the administration of state or districtwide assessments of student achievement that are needed in order for the child to participate in such assessments (If the IEP team determines that the child will not participate, a statement of why that assessment or part of the assessment is not appropriate for the child and how the child will be assessed must be included)

- The projected date for beginning the services and the anticipated frequency, location, and duration of the services and modifications.

The IEP is at the heart of the special education process. No child can receive special education or related services without an IEP because it is the IEP that describes specifically the services that are to be provided and how the child's progress is to be evaluated. Additionally, when children have particular needs related to behavior, LEP, communication (e.g., using Braille, sign language, or hearing aids), or assistive technology (e.g., a communication board with synthesized speech for a child with severe cerebral palsy), these needs must be included on the IEP. Moreover, for children who are age 14 and older, the IEP must contain transitioning goals and objectives related to vocational training or independent living, as well as linkages to necessary adult service agencies that will be needed when the child is no longer in school. Finally, parents may request extended school-year services or special summer school programs as provisions on the IEP if they believe their child will regress during the summer months and have to spend extensive time catching up during the subsequent school year. Most importantly, however, the IEP details the extent to which the child will receive an appropriate education that is to the maximum extent possible alongside his or her peers without disabilities.

Placement in the Least Restrictive Environment

The LRE refers to the placement of the child with disabilities in a setting that is with peers without disabilities whenever possible. Placement in the LRE, then, means that children with disabilities are to be placed in segregated settings only when the nature or severity of their disability is such that an appropriate education in the regular classroom can't be achieved with the use of supplementary aids and support services. Supplementary aids, supports, and services include, but are not limited to, hiring a full-time aide to assist a child, placing a special educator in the regular classroom, or giving the general education teacher a reduced class size.

The LRE does not mean, however, that all children with disabilities must be placed in the regular classroom. Instead, this provision of IDEA (1997) implies that a full continuum of service options must be available to meet the unique needs of the individual child with a disability. Thus, for some children, the LRE may indeed be the regular classroom with modifications in assignments or testing, or with the assistance of a full-time aide. For other children with disabilities, the LRE might be a resource room to which the child goes for a specified period of time daily for assistance in reading or mathematics from his or her special education teacher. Still other children may require a self-contained classroom in the public school, a separate special school, or even residential placement in order to receive an appropriate education. The IEP team, including the parents, determines the child's placement along this continuum of service options.

Early Intervention for Preschoolers, Infants, and Toddlers

Part B of IDEA (1997) ensures access to special education for children of school age (i.e., 6 through 21, inclusive) as well as for children ages 3 to 5 in those states having regulations regarding programs for preschoolers with disabilities. As a matter of fact, IDEA permits children age 3 to 5 who have identifiable physical or mental conditions such as cerebral palsy, autism, mental retardation (e.g., Down syndrome), or hearing impairments to receive the appropriate special education and related services. Moreover, children age 3 to 9 can receive preschool or special education services for "developmental delays" if they are experiencing significant cognitive, physical, language, socioemotional, or adaptive delays as defined by their state of residence and as measured by appropriate diagnostic instruments and procedures (see Table 6.1). These services may be provided within the public school building (e.g., "preschool handicapped" programs or assistance for students with "developmental delays" in Grades 1–3) or through another state agency or program.

Part C of IDEA (1997) guarantees access to early intervention services for infants and toddlers from birth through age 2 who are experiencing developmental delays or who have physical or mental conditions with a high probability of resulting in developmental delays. Thus, high-risk or at-risk infants and toddlers and their families may receive assistance from special educators, psychologists, nurses, nutritionists, and other professionals within the home or another community setting including the following services:

- Family training, counseling, and home visits
- Special instruction
- Speech-language pathology and audiology services
- Occupational therapy
- Physical therapy
- Psychological services
- Service coordination across agencies
- Selected medical services (i.e., those for diagnostic or evaluation purposes only)
- Early identification, screening, and assessment services
- Health services necessary to enable the infant or toddler to benefit from the other early intervention services provided
- Social work services
- Vision services
- Assistive technology devices and services
- Transportation and related costs necessary to enable an infant or toddler and the family to receive another service previously described.

Such early intervention services are actually intended as *prevention* services. That is, they are designed to prevent additional deficits in children as they grow and to reduce the impact of early risk factors on a child's later development. For example, children with visual impairments can be stimulated to explore their environment from birth onward and children with orthopedic impairments can be given physical therapy to improve their muscle tone, strength, and range of motion, thereby enhancing later motor skills. Similarly, children with mental retardation due to Down syndrome can receive early and intensive stimulation to maximize cognitive and language development. When early intervention services are comprehensive, coordinated, individualized, and focused on family involvement, they do produce significant gains for youngsters and lessen the effects of the disability on the child as he or she enters the school years (Guralnick, 1997).

Early intervention services are specified on an Individualized Family Service Plan (IFSP), a document much like the IEP used by the schools. The IFSP outlines the locations and types of services to be provided to the infant or toddler as well as to his or family. In addition, the IFSP lists the family's strengths, concerns, resources and needs relative to the child, the goals for the child, and the responsibilities of the various professionals and agencies involved.

Section 504

Sometimes children simply do not "fit" the definitions or criteria set by states and school districts for special education eligibility. Yet, these children still have difficulty learning or participating fully in their classroom. Fortunately, two additional federal laws prohibit discrimination against students with disabilities: Section 504 of the Vocational Rehabilitation Act Amendments of 1973 and the Americans with Disabilities Act (ADA) of 1990. Whereas IDEA (1997) falls under the Department of Education, these two federal laws are under the auspices of the Office of Civil Rights.

The ADA, however, is much broader in scope than Section 504. The ADA protects individuals with disabilities from discrimination throughout their lives in access to employment, buildings, telecommunications, and transportation. On the other hand, Section 504 prohibits discrimination against individuals with disabilities by agencies of state and local government, including of course, the public schools. Both federal laws, however, prohibit discrimination against "otherwise qualified people with disabilities" and use the same broad definition of disability: Any person who has a physical or mental impairment that substantially limits one or more major life activities or has a record of such an impairment or is regarded as having such an impairment. Thus, when children of school age have a disability that limits one of their major life activities (e.g., learning or walking about the school building), they may qualify for protection under Section 504. Moreover, if a child with a disability once was eligible for services under IDEA but is no longer eligible, he or she may be protected by Section 504. Finally, some children have only minor disabilities (e.g., a cleft palette that has been surgically repaired) or no disability at all, yet people still hold stereotypical or negative beliefs about them based on their appearance (Yell, 1998). These children, too, may qualify for protection under Section 504 as children who are "regarded" as having an impairment.

Students qualifying only under Section 504 do not have an IEP. Instead, they have, depending on what the school calls it, an "accommodation plan" or an "access plan" or an "ADA plan" or a "504 plan." This document lists the particular types of accommodations and modifications to be made to enable the child to participate fully in the school and educational program without discrimination. Extended time to take a test, altering a test format, scheduling classes in the same area of the building to reduce walking distance, and providing preferential seating are examples of the accommodations often listed on a Section 504 plan.

Because requirements under Section 504 include education in the LRE, nondiscriminatory evaluation, and parental or procedural safeguards much like those under IDEA (1997), schools often follow the same process for Section 504 as they do for IDEA. That is, when children are struggling to learn or behave in the classroom, teachers, parents, and other professionals begin by working together to solve the problem. When a legitimate referral is made, a multidisciplinary team gathers data and makes a decision regarding whether or not the child is eligible for special education services under IDEA (1997). If the child does not meet the criterion for a disability covered under IDEA, school personnel typically review the collected data to determine whether or not the child might qualify under the broader Section 504 definition of disability. If the child does indeed qualify, parents and school personnel negotiate a Section 504 plan. Additionally, under Section 504 these procedural safeguards and rights to due process extend to disciplinary infractions (i.e., conducting a Manifestation Determination Review) in much the same way as they are handled under IDEA (1997).

According to Yell (1998), the courts have recognized physical conditions such as arthritis, asthma, diabetes, cerebral palsy, epilepsy, and kidney disease as disabilities that may substantially limit a major life activity. In addition, mental conditions such as ADHD (see Chapter 3) may also be considered as impairments covered under Section 504 when they limit a child's major life activity of learning at school. In fact, schools frequently do provide Section 504 plans to children properly diagnosed with ADHD when they do not meet the criterion for learning disabilities, or any other disability covered by IDEA (1997), but are still experiencing substantial difficulty paying attention and performing in the classroom.

▓ SPECIAL SERVICES AND SPECIAL ISSUES OF INTERCOUNTRY ADOPTION

Children of intercountry adoption, particularly those adopted from institutionalized environments at age 2 or beyond, constitute a high-risk population considered by experts to be "special needs" youngsters (Babb & Laws, 1997; Bascom & McKelvey, 1997; Groze & Ileana, 1996). Poor prenatal care, maternal alcohol or substance abuse, inadequate nutrition and health care, neglect, emotional trauma, limited stimulation, and other factors interact to produce the delayed language, cognitive, motor, and socioemotional skills that frequently accompany institutionalization. As a result, at the time of adoption the individual child may have a developmental age well below that of his or her chronological age. Moreover, unlike the "typical" ESL learner, children of intercountry adoption usually lose their first language while simultaneously learning English. Such a complex background certainly makes determining the cause of learning and/ or behavioral problems quite difficult. School professionals are hard pressed to figure out if the difficulties are due to slower, but "normal," ESL learning (Pearson, 2001), to lack of learning opportunities, to adjustment to adoption and a new culture, to a true disability, or to some other unknown cause.

Although some children will make good progress on their adoption, taking a wait and see approach to the needs of many others may ultimately create even greater delays in their language and literacy development, cognitive or motor ability, or socioemotional competence (Gindis, 1998; Pearson, 2001). Unfortunately, however, school professionals simply do not know how to evaluate or meet the needs of children of intercountry adoption, and even those states having the largest populations of these children (i.e., New York, California,

Pennsylvania, Illinois, New Jersey) have no written guidelines to assist parents or teachers. Thus, children of intercountry adoption may be at risk either for denial of needed special education services or for inappropriate placement in a special education program when such a placement is not really warranted.

For example, unless children of intercountry adoption have obvious physical or cognitive disabilities, schools may refuse to evaluate them for special education eligibility until they have been through a period of time the school considers sufficient to adjust to a new environment and learn to speak English. Although adjustment and learning to understand and speak English are important considerations, parents and teachers who take the wait and see approach may realize after 1 or more years that the child has fallen even farther behind his or her chronological age mates and that valuable time has been lost. *Instead, parents, classroom teachers, special educators, speech-language professionals, and teachers of ESL must collaborate as a team and as early as possible following adoption to consider the whole child and his or her life profile* including such factors as the following:

A. Adoption History

1. What, if anything, is known about the child's prenatal care and birth (e.g., birth weight, gestation period, birth traumas, birth date)?

2. What, if anything, is known about the child's birth mother (e.g., how many pregnancies, age of birth mother, alcohol or substance abuse)?

3. Was the child in an orphanage, and if so, for how long?

4. According to the child's parents, what was the perceived level of care (e.g., nutrition, health services, staff to child ratio, and affection) received in the orphanage?

5. Was the child a "favorite" of orphanage staff?

6. Did the child experience trauma (e.g., war or physical abuse) prior to his or adoption?

B. Medical History

1. Are medical conditions (e.g., a hearing loss due to middle ear infections) noted in the child's records, and if so, were these corroborated by physicians in the United States following adoption?

2. Did the physicians detect any additional medical concerns (e.g., elevated lead levels or severe allergies) following adoption?

3. What do physicians say regarding the child's height and weight and his or her overall pattern of health and growth?

C. Language History

1. At the time of adoption, was the child using and responding to his or her first language at an age-appropriate level?

2. Had the child become literate (i.e., learned to read or write) in his or her first language before adoption?

3. How similar was the first language to English (e.g., a "phonetically regular" language, one with many "irregularities," or one dependent on intonations)?

4. Did the child still hear the first language after arriving in the United States, and if not, how quickly did he or she lose the original language and begin to respond to English?

5. How rapidly is the child gaining increasingly complex skills in understanding and using spoken English?

D. Developmental History

1. Did the child have age-appropriate gross and fine motor skills at the time of adoption, and if not, how rapidly is the child attaining these skills given improved nutrition and stimulation?

2. How rapidly does the child learn new concepts or skills (e.g., names of objects, colors, or numbers) when these are demonstrated?

3. Does the child quickly imitate what he or she observes and then transfer or apply this information to new situations?

4. Does the child appear to enjoy and seek out new information and learning opportunities?

5. Does the child "play" easily and spontaneously?

E. Socioemotional History

1. How "smooth" was the transition from the child's orphanage or birth country to his or her postadoption family life?

2. Did the child exhibit frequent and/or extreme temper tantrums following adoption, and if so, are these continuing or decreasing in frequency and intensity?

3. Does the child sleep regularly through the night?

4. Has the child "bonded" or "attached" to his or her parents?

5. Does the child avoid other adults or other children or approach them willingly (e.g., Is the child shy and withdrawn or curious and outgoing? Has the child made several friends?)?

6. Is the child able to focus and sustain his or her attention in an age-appropriate way?

7. Does the child react in an unusual or fearful manner to "ordinary" events (e.g., getting dirty, children swinging on the playground, being approached by an animal, being bumped or touched by others, etc.)?

8. How easily does the child handle changes in daily routines?

9. Does he or she need a high degree of structure and supervision?

Throughout this initial evaluation, the team must consider the appropriateness of any tests or standardized assessments that might have been used. Recall that eligibility for special education services under IDEA (1997) must be determined using tests that are valid and that are given in a manner that will not be biased by language, culture, or disability. Traditional tests and formal assessments, therefore, may not be available in the child's native language and bilingual professionals in that language may be unavailable. Moreover, children with limited backgrounds such as those adopted from institutions abroad are not included in the sample of children on which these tests were "normed" and they simply do not have the experiential history to perform successfully on many of these "traditional" measures. For example, when Olivia's mother (see Chapters 1 and 7) took her at age 2 to be evaluated at a developmental screening conducted as a part of child find by the early intervention specialists in her local school district, Olivia "failed" some sections of the test. When presented with a simple black-and-white line drawing of a bird on a partial branch and asked "What's this?", Olivia responded with "broke" instead of "bird." She obviously understood an important concept (i.e., the branch appeared to be broken to her because it disappeared off the side of the examiner's stimulus page) but she did not properly identify the object, bird. Given Olivia's history and limited time of only 8 months in the United States, the examiner told her mother that she believed that Olivia was developing at an appropriate pace and catching up to her chronological-age peers on motor and cognitive skills. She cautioned her mother, however, to bring Olivia back to the screening program in a few months to be reevaluated on the "failed" portions of the test such as language development.

Similarly, Schell-Frank (2000) described a parent's frustration with obtaining appropriate testing for her son. This parent clearly believes that her child is capable of learning and she accurately recognizes that standardized testing is inappropriate. Yet, she is frustrated in her attempts to gain the necessary assistance for her son unless she grants permission for the school to administer the tests:

> I put him into first grade when he came at age eight. He had no English and little school experience. He has done beautifully learning verbal English. However, he went into second grade unable to read, which completely threw his teacher for a loop. His actual comprehension of English at that point was minimal due to the enormity of the task. He had volumes to learn in every aspect of his life. The teacher was furious because I refused to have him tested. I knew he couldn't test, and they wanted to do this to place him in special education. (Schell-Frank, 2000, p. 56)

Unless school professionals carefully consider the nature of standardized tests and their appropriateness for children of intercountry adoption, these children may "fail" the tests and, subsequently, be placed inappropriately in special education programs such as those for children having cognitive disabilities like mental retardation or learning disabilities. Instead, school professionals should place a reduced emphasis on standardized test data and pay increased attention to performance-based assessment and information from the child's life history and profile including the adoption, medical, language, developmental, and socioemotional factors previously discussed. That is, school professionals serving children of intercountry adoption must listen to parents and to their explanations of what their children are able to do and how rapidly they are able to learn to do it.

On the other hand, without special education or some other form of assistance children of intercountry adoption may not be able to catch up on their own. The degree of early deprivation and the low level of language development experienced by so many of these children may make it far more difficult for them to overcome obstacles and close the learning gap on their own than for other low achieving children born in the United States. For these children, time and early intervention are critical.

Thus, parents may sometimes need to accept labels such as "mental retardation" or "mild autism" that don't really seem to fit their child in order to get the special assistance that could help him or her (Schell-Frank, 2000). Parents, however, must ensure that the IEP is appropriate and that their youngster will receive *intensified instruction designed to address his or her unique needs*. As a matter of fact, most children of intercountry adoption who join their families while under the age of three should be considered eligible for early intervention services under IDEA (1997). These are certainly children with identified physical or mental conditions, measurable developmental delays, or *a high risk* of later experiencing developmental delays due to early environmental circumstances and life events. Moreover, many preschool children of intercountry adoption who enter the United States at ages 3 through 5 do indeed evidence significant developmental delays. These children, too, would benefit from the label "developmentally delayed" if they could receive intensified programs as preschoolers or school-age youngsters with disabilities. Such early intensified services have the potential to help the child catch up with chronological-age peers, lessen the impact of early deprivation, reduce failure and frustration, and, hopefully, prevent more stigmatizing special education labels at a later time.

※ CONCLUSION

Children of intercountry adoption are at risk for learning and behavioral difficulties in school. They are also at risk both for over- and underrepresentation in special education programs. School professionals do not know how to evaluate these children or how to meet their needs. Furthermore, school districts and state departments of education are hesitant to "categorize" this group of children as in need of special education services, preferring instead to offer ESL or to wait and see. Although this reluctance is well intended, its result is that parents and school personnel needlessly waste time and energy seeking help for some children of intercountry adoption while meeting with little or no success.

Given the unique backgrounds of children of intercountry adoption, school professionals are advised not to apply a rigid set of existing standards to these youngsters. They most assuredly will not be appropriately evaluated or served through conventional practices. Rather, the following guidelines for serving children of intercountry adoption are offered for consideration by school personnel:

1. Work to reduce or eliminate competing school requirements that prevent children of intercountry adoption from receiving early evaluations for special education eligibility. For example, rules specifying that children must be in ESL programs for 1 year or that they must "test out" of ESL before they can be evaluated for special

education are barriers to early and necessary services for some children.

2. Use performance-based assessment and observational data in the decision-making process instead of relying primarily on standardized test scores and comparisons. Use a test, teach, and test again sequence to determine how quickly the child learns and responds to instruction.

3. Listen carefully to the child's parents and weigh the child's life profile, preadoption experiences, and pattern of learning as much, if not more than, information obtained through standard testing procedures.

4. Consider the young child (i.e., ages 0–5) to be eligible for early intervention or preschool disability programs when these are available in the state. In addition, consider the child who is ages 6 through 8 to be eligible for services for children with developmental delays in order to intensify instruction and target needs as quickly as possible whenever necessary.

5. Ensure the child is placed with chronological-age peers to the maximum extent possible to provide exposure to positive models of language and behavior.

6. Provide a plan of action similar to an IEP or to a Section 504 plan for children of intercountry adoption. These children may or may not meet the eligibility requirements for special education under IDEA (1997) and they may or may not qualify for services under Section 504. However, they have special and unique needs that may require intense, targeted instruction and collaboration among parents and many different school professionals (e.g., ESL, speech-language, occupational therapy, psychologists, or counselors).

Such complex needs cannot be left solely to chance. Parents and school professionals must work together in a coordinated manner to ensure the best possible outcomes for children of intercountry adoption. When school personnel are willing to meet the needs of all children, including those with complex backgrounds who have been adopted from orphanages abroad, parents do indeed have reason for hope and optimism. More importantly, the thousands of youngsters of intercountry adoption who arrive in the United States each year will have the best possible opportunity to "catch up," grow, develop, and become healthy, independent, and productive citizens.

Chapter 7

Postscript: Laura, Jennifer, and Olivia

C hildren of intercountry adoption, especially those who come from institutionalized backgrounds, face tremendous obstacles. Most of them, however, surprise and please their parents and teachers as they enter school and advance through the grades! Despite their many unique needs, these children can learn and make good progress. This progress, however, is often dependent on the concerted efforts, collaboration, and determination of parents, teachers, and even the children themselves. Witness, for example, the continuing stories of Laura, Jennifer, and Olivia (see Chapter 1).

✿ LAURA

Laura, at age 9 years, 7 months, is currently in a regular fourth-grade classroom. Her mother states that she worked with Laura over the summer between third and fourth grades on reading, spelling, and mathematics and that Laura now comes home from school every day "very happy." Although Laura claims she "hates" math, her teacher said in a recent conference with her mother that math is Laura's strongest subject. Laura is still having difficulty with some basic math concepts, but she is able to "stay up with the class" on most of the activities.

Laura is still struggling, however, in reading and spelling. Her teacher tested her at the start of the fourth grade and found that she was reading at one level below her current grade placement. She seems unable to establish her own strategy for decoding new words and tends to get very frustrated when she is reading. She is also having difficulty with reading comprehension; however, her mother believes this is due to Laura's inability to decode the words and not to any cognitive difficulty remembering or understanding what she reads.

Laura's teacher describes her as quiet and attentive in class, but she feels the work is quite challenging for Laura. Her teacher also sees Laura as a "hard worker" who becomes frustrated easily. Laura is starting to "open up" in class now, however, and her teacher is hopeful that she will soon start to make "big gains."

JENNIFER

Jennifer's mother recently attended the annual IEP meeting for her daughter held in her school during mid-October. Jennifer, almost age 9, is now in first grade after attending kindergarten for 2 years. According to her mother, everyone present at the IEP meeting was extremely pleased with Jennifer's progress—Jennifer met and exceeded all of the goals established in her IEP during the last year. She is now reading some easy books and sounding out the spelling of many words. Jennifer is also learning basic math concepts and "keeping up with" the new math skills presented so far in first grade.

Jennifer will continue to receive special education services this year to address some continuing areas of concern. For example, she is still having trouble with the proper word order in sentences, especially for "question-type" sentences. Additionally, her receptive and expressive vocabularies are still smaller than that of most children in the first grade, and Jennifer also continues to have difficulty retelling a story or repeating a series of oral instructions. Finally, Jennifer has a lot of difficulty generalizing concepts beyond the context in which she learned that concept. For example, she learned the names of the coins "penny," "nickel," "dime," and "quarter" in that order. Jennifer can tell the name of the coin and how much each coin is worth as long as the coins are in that order in front of her. If, however, her teacher or her mother takes one of the coins out of the line and asks Jennifer to state the name or value of the coin, she does not know.

To her mother's dismay, this follows many weeks of reviewing the names and values of the coins.

Nevertheless, her mother is quite optimistic. She states that "all in all, Jennifer is doing wonderfully." Furthermore, her mother says, "Her teachers are very impressed with her progress and with her desire to succeed."

✿ OLIVIA

Now home for only a little more than 8 months, Olivia just turned age 2. Olivia's mother recently took her to the free preschool developmental screening offered by the school district in which she lives to determine whether or not Olivia might require early intervention special education services. To the contrary, her mother was quite pleased with the results of Olivia's evaluation.

Olivia can now go up and down steps on her own with alternating feet and she can jump with two feet. She is also beginning to run. Olivia asks for her glasses and wears them! Olivia now has an English vocabulary estimated at about 50 words and she frequently speaks in two-word sentences. Although her words are not always intelligible to others, her parents can clearly understand her when she says sentences such as, "Daddy, where are you?"

According to her mother, Olivia is a happy child who loves to listen to music. She is also beginning to enjoy playing with simple puzzles and blocks. Olivia now sleeps only about 12 hours, instead of 13, each night and she is giving up her morning nap. Her parents are quite pleased that Olivia now tells them when she needs to "go potty." They are saddened, however, that she no longer recognizes or responds to the Chinese words she once knew.

✿ CONCLUSION

Clearly, Laura, Jennifer, and Olivia are children who continue to amaze and delight their parents. Despite an institutionalized background and a change in language and culture, each child is growing, developing, and becoming successful in the eyes of family, teachers, and friends. As suggested by Groze (Groze & Ileana, 1996), perhaps parents and school professionals do indeed have reason for cautious optimism, but only with continued vigilance to ensure that the complex needs of these children are being adequately addressed.

Appendix A: Organizations and Resources

✻ ADVOCACY, RESEARCH, AND SUPPORT

Adoption.Org
Web site: http://www.adoption.org
E-mail: comment@adoption.org

This animated site includes numerous resources and links for anyone interested or involved in adoption. Areas include photo listings of potential parents and children, chat areas, adoption law, birth family search, research, and much more.

Adoptive Families Together (AFT)
Phone: 617–929–3800
Address: 418 Commonwealth Avenue
          Boston, MA 02215
Web site: http://www.adoptivefamilies.org
E-mail: web@adoptivefamilies.org

AFT is a support network designed to strengthen adoptive families by providing a venue for sharing information and experiences.

American Adoption Congress (AAC)
Phone: 202–483–3399

Address: 1025 Connecticut Avenue NW, Suite 1012
　　　　　Washington, DC 20036
Web site: http://www.americanadoptioncongress.org
E-mail: BBetzen@aol.com

The AAC is an international network of individuals, families, and organizations committed to truth in adoption and to reform that protects all those involved from abuse or exploitation.

Child Welfare League of America (CWLA)
Phone: 202–638–2952
Address: 440 First Street NW, Suite 310
　　　　　Washington, DC 20001–2085
Web site: http://www.cwla.org

The CWLA is an association of public and private organizations committed to improving the quality of life for at-risk children and families, especially through the prevention and treatment of child abuse and neglect.

Council for Equal Rights in Adoption (CERA)
Phone: 212–988–0110
Address: 356 East 74th Street, Suite 2
　　　　　New York, NY 10021
Web site: http://www.adoptioncrossroads.org

CERA is a nonprofit, worldwide search and support network for adoptees and birth parents dedicated to the preservation and reunification of families.

Dave Thomas Foundation for Adoption (DTFA)
Phone: 614–764–3100
Address: 4288 West Dublin-Granville Road
　　　　　Dublin, OH 43017
Web site: http://www.davethomasfoundationforadoption.org

The DTFA serves as an advocate for children in the public child welfare system awaiting permanent, loving families. These children may be older, in sibling groups, from minority cultures, or have special needs.

Evan B. Donaldson Adoption Institute
Phone: 212–269–5080
Address: 120 Wall Street, 20th Floor
　　　　　New York, NY 10005–3902
Web site: http://www.adoptioninstitute.org
E-mail: dhays@adoptioninstitute.org

The Evan B. Donaldson Adoption Institute is dedicated to increasing public understanding of adoption and improving adoption policy and practice.

International Adoption Alliance
Web site: http://www.i-a-a.org
E-mail: interadopt@home.com

The International Adoption Alliance is a nonprofit organization that attempts to provide cultural resources for transcultural families, to advocate for these families, and to increase awareness of waiting children and the programs that serve them.

International Concerns Committee for Children (ICCC)
Phone: 303–494–8333
Address: 911 Cypress Drive
        Boulder, CO 80303
Web site: http://www.iccadopt.org
E-mail: icc@boulder.net

The ICC is a charitable and educational organization created to provide the public with information concerning the availability of waiting children, adoption procedures, and international adoption issues.

Joint Council on International Children's Services (JCICS)
Phone: 202–429–0400
Address: 1320 Nineteenth Street NW, Suite 200
        Washington, DC 20036
Web site: http://www.jcics.org
E-mail: SKaufman@jcics.org

The JCICS is an affiliation of licensed, nonprofit international adoption agencies, parent groups, advocacy organizations, and individuals.

National Adoption Foundation (NAF)
Phone: 203–791–3811
Address: 100 Mill Plain Road
        Danbury, CT 06811
Web site: http://www.nafadopt.org
E-mail: info@nafadopt.org

The NAF was established by adoptive families to provide financial assistance, services, and support directly to adoptive families before, during, and after the adoption process.

National Adoption Information Clearinghouse (NAIC)
Phone: 888–251–0075

Address: 33 C Street, SW
          Washington, DC 20447
Web site: http://www.calib.com/naic
E-mail: naic@calib.com

The NAIC provides information on all aspects of adoption for professionals, policymakers, and the general public. Services include technical assistance, publications, resource databases, and legislation information.

National Council for Adoption (NCFA)
Phone: 202–328–1200
Address: 1930 Seventeenth Street, NW
          Washington, DC 20009–6207
Web site: http://www.ncfa-usa.org/home.html
E-mail: ncfa@ncfa-usa.org

The NCFA is a charitable organization that helps adoptive parents locate information on the adoption process, agencies, attorneys, and related literature.

National Council for Single Adoptive Parents
Phone: 202–966–6367
Address: PO Box 55
          Wharton, NJ 07885
Web site: http://www.adopting.org/ncsap.html
E-mail: ncsap@hotmail.com

The National Council for Single Adoptive Parents offers advice and support for single men and women who want to adopt. The council also publishes a comprehensive handbook for adoptive single parents.

New Roots
Phone: 614–470–0846
Address: PO Box 1495
          Columbus, OH 43214
Web site: http://www.simplyliving.org/newroots

New Roots is a nonprofit membership organization that provides support, education, and encouragement for families with adopted children, those in the process of adopting, and those considering adoption.

North American Council on Adoptable Children (NACAC)
Phone: 651–644–3036
Address: 970 Raymond Avenue, Suite 106
          St. Paul, MN 55114

Web site: http://www.nacac.org
E-mail: info@nacac.org

The NACAC is committed to finding homes for every waiting child, particularly older children, those in sibling groups, and those with other special needs.

Pact, An Adoption Alliance
Phone: 415–221–6957
Address: 1700 Montgomery Street, Suite 111
        San Francisco, CA 94111
Web site: http://www.pactadopt.org
E-mail: info@pactadopt.org

Pact is a nonprofit organization designed to ensure that every child feels wanted, honored, and loved. The organization especially promotes programs for children of color and their families.

Rainbow Kids: An International Adoption Publication
Web site: http://www.rainbowkids.com
E-mail: rbowkids@aol.com

Rainbow Kids is a monthly online adoption publication that focuses on international adoption issues. The site also offers a number of helpful links and resources for those considering international adoption.

Resources for Adoptive Parents (RAP)
Phone: 612–926–6959
Address: 3381 Gorham Avenue, Suite 212
        Minneapolis, MN 55416

RAP sponsors educational meetings, support groups, respite care, a lending library, and counseling and consulting for current and prospective adoptive parents.

Zero to Three: National Center for Infants, Toddlers, and Families
Phone: 202–638–1144
Address: 734 15th Street NW, Suite 1000
        Washington, DC 20005–1013
Web site: http://www.zerotothree.org
E-mail: 0to3@zerotothree.org

Zero to Three is a national nonprofit organization designed to promote the healthy development of infants and toddlers by supporting families, professionals, and communities.

✼ BIRTH COUNTRY CONNECTIONS

Adoption Travel.com
Web site: http://www.adoptiontravel.com

This Web site provides resources, such as travel tips and links to various agencies, for families wishing to travel in order to adopt internationally or revisit their child's birth country.

AdoptShoppe
Phone: 301–464–9423
Address: PO Box 841
        Bowie, MD 20718–0841
Web site: http://www.adoptshoppe.com
E-mail: info@adoptshoppe.com

AdoptShoppe is a source where adoptive parents may find items of usefulness, value, and beauty for their children. Most of the products relate to Asian countries, but there is also a section on domestic adoptions.

Americans Support Heritage for Adoptees (ASHA, Inc.)
Phone: 541–385–0746
Address: 65925 61st Street
        Bend, OR 97701–8701
Web site: http://www.oregontrail.net/india/
E-mail: asha@apaynet.com

ASHA, Inc. is dedicated to education and support of adopted children and their families. The organization provides ethnic goods from India to celebrate diversity and keep families connected to India.

Central Adoption Resource Agency (CARA)
Phone: 091–011–610–9193
Address: Ministry of Social Justice and Empowerment (India)
        West Block 8, Wing-2, 2nd Floor,
        R.K. Puram, New Delhi-110 066
        India
Web site: http://www.adoptionindia.nic.in
E-mail: cara@bol.net.in

CARA is an autonomous body under the Ministry of Social Justice and Empowerment in India. The agency was formed to ensure that all adoptions are legal and to protect children from exploitation.

ChinaSprout, Inc.
Phone: 718–439–7278

Address: 169 54th Street, Suite 10
          Brooklyn, NY 11220
Web site: http://www.chinasprout.com/index.html

ChinaSprout, Inc. provides numerous products and services relating to China. The website is a truly comprehensive resource on Chinese and Chinese-American culture.

Families for Russian and Ukrainian Adoption (FRUA)
Phone: 703–560–6184
Address: PO Box 2944
          Merrifield VA, 22116
Web site: http://www.frua.org

FRUA is a nonprofit support for adoptive families with children from the former Soviet Union. Along with the support of other similar families, the organization also offers cultural events, a regular newsletter, and a forum for advocacy.

Families with Children from China (FCC)
Web site: http://www.fwcc.org

FCC provides a support network for families who have adopted or are considering adopting from China. The Web site offers various resources and links to relevant information. Check the Web site to find your nearest local chapter.

Families with Children from Viet Nam (FCV)
Web site: http://www.fcvn.org

FCV is a support network for families who have adopted or are considering adopting from Vietnam. The Web site offers resources and links to information on adopting, parenting, personal stories, and a listing of local chapters.

ICHILD: India Adoption Resources
Web site: http://www.ichild.org
E-mail: bethpk@ichild.org

ICHILD's Web site and mailing lists are designed to offer a source of inspiration, information, support, and resources for those interested in adoption from India.

International Mission of Hope
Phone: 970–226–0147
Address: PO Box 735
          Fort Collins, CO 80522–0735

Web site: http://www.imh-vn.org
E-mail: imh@imh-vn.org

IMH is dedicated to helping the people of Vietnam care for their children, their land and their heritage. The mission also facilitates families interested in adopting from Vietnam.

Korean Adoptee Homepage (Global Korean League)
Web site: http://www.adoptee.com/BBS/Main
E-mail: kap@adoptee.com

This Web site offers an opinion forum and discussion area for Korean adoptees to gather and unify, creating a stronger sense of kinship.

Latin American Parents Association (LAPA)
Phone: 516–752–0086
Address: PO Box 72
        Seaford, NY 11783
Web site: http://www.lapa.com

LAPA is a volunteer association of adoptive parents committed to supporting and aiding those who have or are seeking to adopt from Latin American countries.

Multicultural Kids
Phone: 847–991–2919
Address: PO Box 757
        Palatine, IL 60078–0757
Web site: http://www.multiculturalkids.com
E-mail: mck@mediaone.net

Multicultural Kids provides materials for children in the home and classroom that can be used to increase a child's knowledge of him or herself and others, enhancing self-esteem while fostering tolerance and appreciation of diversity.

Paraguay Adoption Resources
Phone: 707–763–6835
Address: 1724 Burgundy Court
        Petaluma, CA 94954
Web site: http://www.pyadopt.org
E-mail: Paraguay@wco.com

Paraguay Adoption Resources offers a great deal of information for families considering adopting from Paraguay. The Web site, PYadopt.org, provides numerous educational and cultural resources and links.

Stars of David International, Inc.
Phone: 800–STAR–349
Address: PO Box 573
       Woodbury, NJ 08096–0573
Web site: http://www.starsofdavid.org
E-mail: starsdavid@aol.com

Stars of David is a nonprofit information and support network for Jewish and interfaith adoptive families, as well as birth parents, adoptees, adoptive parents, prospective parents, single parents, grandparents, interfaith couples, and transracial and transcultural families.

Ties Program
Phone: 800–398–3676
Address: 10520 W. Bluemound Road
       Wauwatosa, WI 53226
Web site: http://www.AdoptiveFamilyTravel.com
E-mail: info@adoptivefamilytravel.com

The Ties Program helps adoptive families visit their child's birth country to see the sights, experience the culture, and reconnect with significant people and places related to their adoption.

Treasures of the Rodina
Phone: 770–619–3019
Address: 10440 Windsor Park Drive
       Apharetta, GA 30022
Web site: http://www.rodinatreasures.com
E-mail: TotRodina@aol.com

Treasures of the Rodina offers a number of handcrafted works of art from Russia. The company can even have a Russian artist produce Matroishkas (stacking dolls) in the likeness of your family.

❈ CHILDREN WITH SPECIAL NEEDS

American Academy of Child and Adolescent Psychiatry (AACAP)
Phone: 202–966–7300
Address: 3615 Wisconsin Avenue, NW
       Washington, DC 20016–3007
Web site: http://www.aacap.org

The AACAP is a national nonprofit professional medical association dedicated to treating and improving the quality of life for children, adolescents, and families affected by mental, behavioral, and developmental disorders.

American Association for Gifted Children (AAGC)
Phone: 919–783–6152
Address: PO Box 90270
        Durham, North Carolina 27708–0270
Web site: http://www.aagc.org

The AAGC is an advocacy organization for gifted children. Although it provides information to educational and medical professionals, the AAGC is focused on providing information to help parents raise gifted children.

American Association on Mental Retardation (AAMR)
Phone: 800–424–3688
Address: 444 North Capitol Street NW, Suite 846
        Washington, DC 20001–1512
Web site: http://www.aamr.org/index.shtml
E-mail: info@aamr.org

The AAMR promotes progressive policies, sound research, effective practices, and universal human rights for people with intellectual disabilities.

American Occupational Therapy Association, Inc. (AOTA)
Phone: 800–668–8255
        800–377–8555 (TDD)
Address: PO Box 31220
        Bethesda, MD 20824–1220
Web site: http://www.aota.org

AOTA is a national professional association of occupational therapists and assistants working together to advance and promote the field of occupational therapy.

American Speech-Language-Hearing Association (ASHA)
Phone: 800–638–8255
        301–897–5700 (Voice/TTD)
Address: 10801 Rockville Pike
        Rockville, MD 20852
Web site: http://www.asha.org
E-mail: irc@asha.org

ASHA is the primary association of speech, language, and hearing professionals. Its mission is to ensure that anyone with a speech, language, or hearing disorder may have access to quality communication services.

The Arc
Phone: 800–433–5255
      817–277–0533 (TDD)
Address: 500 East Border Street, Suite 300
      Arlington, TX 76010
Web site: http://www.thearc.org
E-mail: thearc@metronet.com

The Arc is the national organization of and for people with mental retardation and related developmental disorders. Its mission is to improve the quality of life for these people and to prevent the causes and effects of mental retardation.

Association for Treatment and Training in the Attachment of Children (AT-
   TACh)
Phone: 803–251–0120
Address: PO Box 11347
      Columbia, SC 29211
Web site: http://www.attach.org
E-mail: info@attach.org

ATTACh is an international coalition of professionals and individuals involved with children who have attachment difficulties. ATTACh is committed to promoting the identification of attachment issues and effective interventions.

Attachment Disorder Parents Network (ADPN)
Address: PO Box 18475
      Boulder, CO 80308

The ADPN is a support network for families of children with attachment disorders. The group works to inform the public and help families get the information and services they need.

Children and Adults with Attention Deficit Disorder (CHADD)
Phone: 800–233–4050
Address: 499 Northwest 70th Avenue, Suite 308
      Plantation, FL 33317
Web site: http://www.chadd.org
E-mail: national@chadd.org

CHADD is a national nonprofit organization representing individuals with ADHD. The organization works to improve the lives of people with ADHD through education, advocacy, and support.

Childswork/Childsplay
Phone: 800–962–1141

Address: PO Box 760
        Plainview, NY 11803–0760
Web site: http://www.childswork.com

Childswork/Childsplay is a company that provides information, resources, and products designed to address the social and emotional
needs of children and adolescents, especially through play.

Council for Children with Behavioral Disorders (CCBD)
Address: 1920 Association Drive
        Reston, VA 22091
Web site: http://www.ccbd.net/index.cfm

The CCBD is the official division of the Council for Exceptional Children (CEC) committed to promoting and facilitating the education
and general welfare of children and youth with emotional or behavioral disorders.

Council for Exceptional Children (CEC)
Phone: 888–CEC–SPED
        703–264–9446 (TTY)
Address: 1110 North Glebe Road, Suite 300
        Arlington, VA 22201–5704
Web site: http://www.cec.sped.org
E-mail: service@cec.sped.org

The CEC is an international professional organization dedicated to
improving educational outcomes for individuals with exceptionalities,
students with disabilities, and/or the gifted.

Council for Learning Disabilities (CLD)
Phone: 913–492–8755
Address: PO Box 40303
        Overland Park, KS 62204
Web site: http://www.cldinternational.org

The CLD is an international organization concerned about issues related to students with LD. Its primary goal is to build a better future
for students with LD.

Developmental Delay Resources (DDR)
Phone: 301–652–2263
Address: 4401 East-West Highway, Suite 207
        Bethesda, MD 20814
Web site: http://www.devdelay.org

DDR is a nonprofit organization dedicated to meeting the needs of those working with children who have developmental delays. The organization also provides a support network for parents and professionals.

Families and Advocates Partnership for Education (FAPE)
Phone: 888–248–0822
Address: 8161 Normandale Boulevard
        Minneapolis, MN 55437
Web site: http://www.fape.org
E-mail: fape@pacer.org

FAPE is a project that aims to inform and educate families and advocates about the IDEA of 1997. The partnership helps to ensure that changes in IDEA are effectively understood and put into practice.

Federation of Families for Children's Mental Health
Phone: 703–684–7710
Address: 1021 Prince Street
        Alexandria, VA 22314
Web site: http://www.ffcmh.org

The Federation of Families for Children's Mental Health is a national parent-run organization focused on the needs of children and youth with emotional, behavioral, or mental disorders and their families.

Learning Disabilities Association of America, Inc. (LDA)
Phone: 412–341–1515
Address: 4156 Library Road
        Pittsburgh, PA 15234
Web site: http://www.ldanatl.org
E-mail: ldanatl@usaor.net

LDA is a nonprofit volunteer organization advocating for individuals with learning disabilities. The association is devoted to defining and finding solutions for the broad spectrum of learning disabilities.

National Alliance for Mentally Ill (NAMI)
Phone: 800–950-NAMI (6264)
Address: Colonial Place Three
        2107 Wilson Boulevard, Suite 300
        Arlington, VA 22201
Web site: http://www.nami.org

NAMI is a nonprofit self-help, support, and advocacy organization of consumers, families, and friends of people with severe mental illnesses.

National Association for Gifted Children (NAGC)
Phone: 202–785–4268
Address: 1707 L Street NW, Suite 550
        Washington, DC 20036
Web site: http://www.nagc.org
E-mail: nagc@nagc.org

NAGC is a nonprofit organization of parents, educators, profession-als, and community leaders who unite to address the unique needs of all children and youth with potential or demonstrated gifts and talents.

National Center for Learning Disabilities (NCLD)
Phone: 888–575–7373
Address: 381 Park Avenue South, Suite 1401
        New York, NY 10016
Web site: http://www.ncld.org

The NCLD works to increase opportunities for all individuals with learning disabilities to achieve their potential. The center offers nu-merous solutions that help people with LD participate fully in society.

National Clearinghouse on Child Abuse and Neglect Information
Phone: 800–394–3366
Address: PO Box 1182
        Washington, DC 20013–1182
Web site: http://www.calib.com/nccanch
E-mail: nccanch@calib.com

The Clearinghouse provides information, products, and technical as-sistance services related to child welfare issues, such as research, sta-tistics, state laws, and other resources.

National Information Center for Children and Youth with Disabilities
  (NICHCY)
Phone: 800–695–0285
Address: PO Box 1492
        Washington, DC 20013
Web site: http://www.nichcy.org
E-mail: nichcy@aed.org

NICHCY is the national information and referral center that provides information on disabilities and disability-related issues for families, educators, and other professionals.

National Organization of Fetal Alcohol Syndrome (NOFAS)
Phone: 800–66-NOFAS

Address: 216 G Street, NE
            Washington, DC 20002
Web site: http://www.nofas.org
E-mail: information@nofas.org

NOFAS is a nonprofit organization dedicated to eliminating birth defects caused by alcohol consumption during pregnancy and improving the quality of life for those individuals and families affected by FAS.

Parent Advocacy Coalition for Educational Rights (PACER)
Phone: 952–838–9000
            952–838–0190 (TTY)
Address: 8161 Normandale Boulevard
            Minneapolis, MN 55437
Web site: http://www.pacer.org
E-mail: pacer@pacer.org

PACER, which is based on the concept of parents helping parents, expands opportunities and enhances the quality of life of children and young adults with disabilities as well as their families.

Parent Educational Advocacy Training Center (PEATC)
Phone: 703–923–0010
Address: 6320 Augusta Drive
            Springfield, VA 22150
Web site: http://www.peatc.org
E-mail: partners@peatc.org

PEATC assists families of children with disabilities through education, information, and training. PEATC works to build partnerships between parents and professionals to promote success in school and community life.

Parent Network for the Post-Institutionalized Child (PNPIC)
Phone: 412–222–1776
Address: PO Box 613
            Meadow Lands, PA 15347
Web site: http://www.pnpic.org
E-mail: info@pnpic.org

PNPIC is a family support network devoted to understanding the medical, developmental, emotional, and educational needs of children adopted from hospitals, orphanages, and institutions throughout the world.

Pediatric Therapy Network
Phone: 310–328–0276
Address: 1815 West 213th Street, Suite 140
Torrance, CA 90501
Web site: http://www.pediatrictherapy.com
E-mail: PTN_WEB@hotmail.com

The Pediatric Therapy Network is a nonprofit network of therapists, parents, and professionals committed to helping children with various disabilities. This organization sponsors therapy, early intervention, day camp, and after-school programs.

Post Traumatic Stress Disorder Alliance
Phone: 877–507–PTSD (7873)
Web site: http://www.ptsdalliance.org/home2.html
E-mail: info@ptsdalliance.org

The PTSD Alliance is a multidisciplinary group of professional and advocacy organizations that works to provide educational resources to increase awareness and promote a better understanding of the prevalence, diagnosis, and treatment of PTSD.

Recordings for the Blind and Dyslexic (RFB&D)
Phone: 800–221–4792
Address: 20 Roszel Road
Princeton, NJ 08540
Web site: http://www.rfbd.org

RFB&D provides materials for all people who cannot effectively read standard print because of a visual, perceptual, or other physical disability.

Research & Training Center on Family Support and Children's Mental Health
Phone: 503–725–4040
Address: Portland State University
PO Box 751
Portland, OR 97207–0751
Web site: http://www.rtc.pdx.edu
E-mail: rtcinfo@rri.pdx.edu

The center is dedicated to promoting effective community-based, culturally competent, family-centered services for families and their children who may be affected by mental, emotional, or behavioral disorders.

Sensory Integration International (SII)
Phone: 310–320–2335
Address: 1514 Cabrillo Avenue
         Torrence, CA 90501
Web site: http://www.sensoryint.com
E-mail: info@sensoryint.com

The goal of SII is to improve the quality of life for persons with sensory processing disorders. The organization promotes education about the impacts of inadequate sensory processing and advocates early intervention.

Sibling Support Project
The Sibling Support Project
Phone: 206–368–4911
Address: Children's Hospital and Medical Center
         PO Box 5371, CL-09
         Seattle, WA 98105
Web site: http://www.seattlechildrens.org/sibsupp
E-mail: mdj9@qwest.net

The Sibling Support Project is a program dedicated to the interests of brothers and sisters of people with special needs. The project's primary goal is to increase the availability of peer support and education programs.

Spaulding—National Resource Center on Special Needs Adoption
Phone: 248–443–7080
Address: 16250 Northland Drive, Suite 120
         Southfield, MI 48075
Web site: http://www.spaulding.org
E-mail: sfc@spaulding.org

Spaulding believes that every child is adoptable and deserves a permanent family. The center provides help to waiting children and support services for their adoptive, foster, and kinship families.

✽ GOVERNMENT OFFICES

Administration for Children and Families (ACF)
Phone: 202–401–9215
Address: 370 Promenade
         Washington, DC 20047
Web site: http://www.acf.dhhs.gov

The ACF is responsible for federal programs that promote the economic and social well-being of families, children, individuals, and communities.

Americans with Disabilities Act (ADA) Office
Phone: 202–514–0301
        202–514–0383 (TTD)
Address: U.S. Dept. of Justice, Civil Rights Division
        PO Box 66118
        Washington, DC 20035–6118
Web site: http://www.usdoj.gov/crt/ada/adahom1.htm

The ADA Office is designed to provide information about the Americans with Disabilities Act.

Immigration and Naturalization Service (INS)
Phone: 800–375–5283
        800–767–1833 (TTY)
Web site: http://www.ins.gov/graphics/index.htm

The INS is responsible for enforcing the laws regulating the admission of foreign-born persons to the United States and for administering various immigration benefits, including the naturalization of qualified applicants for U.S. citizenship.

Office of Children's Issues
Phone: 202–736–7000
Address: U.S. Department of State
        2401 E Street, N.W., Room L127
        Washington, DC 20037
Web site: http://travel.state.gov/children's_issues.html

The Office of Children's Issues coordinates policy and provides general information and assistance regarding international adoption.

National Institute of Mental Health (NIMH)
Phone: 301–443–4513
Address: 5600 Fischers Lane
        Bethesda, MD 20857
Web site: http://www.nimh.nih.gov

NIMH works to diminish the burden of mental illness through research. NIMH offers information on current, past, and future research concerning mental illness.

❋ INTERNATIONAL ADOPTION CLINICS

Evaluation Center for Adoption at Schneider Children's Hospital
Phone: 718–470–4000
Address: 269–01 76th Avenue, Suite 139
New York, NY 11040
Web site: http://www.adoption.com/adesman

The Evaluation Center helps parents make an informed decision when considering adoption through counseling, based on a thorough medical and developmental evaluation of the child using available materials and related information.

International Adoption Center at Children's Hospital Medical Center of
    Cincinnati
Phone: 800–344–2462
Address: 3333 Burnet Avenue
        Cincinnati, OH 45229–3039
Web site: http://www.cincinnatichildrens.org/programs_services/308

The center offers preadoption consultations, postadoption evaluations, community outreach, and research concerning international adoption.

International Adoption Clinic at The Floating Hospital for Children
Phone: 617–636–8121
Address: New England Medical Center
        750 Washington Street
        Boston, MA 02111
Web site: http://polaris.nemc.org/home/overview/childrens.htm

The clinic specializes in the evaluation of medical, developmental, and nutritional problems among internationally adopted children.

International Adoption Clinic at University of Minnesota
Phone: 612–624–1164
Address: Mayo Mail Code #211
        420 Delaware Street SE
        Minneapolis, MN 55455
Web site: http://www.peds.umn.edu/IAC
E-mail: iac@tc.umn.edu

The clinic offers counseling for prospective adoptive parents, screening for adopted children, and ongoing follow-up and referrals. The clinic also acts as a center for research on internationally adopted children and institutionalization.

International Adoptions Clinic at Hasbro Children's Hospital
Phone: 401–444–8360
Address: Boris Skurkovich, M.D.
　　　　　Division of Pediatric ID
　　　　　Rhode Island Hospital
　　　　　593 Eddy Street
　　　　　Providence, RI 02903
Web site: http://www.adoptionsinternational.com
E-mail: adopt@adoptionsinternational.com

The clinic provides medical counseling and preadoption services, including a review of medical records, photographs, videotapes, correspondence regarding concerns and questions, and a written medical opinion.

※ LEGAL INFORMATION

American Academy of Adoption Attorneys (AAAA)
Phone: 202–832–2222
Address: PO Box 33053
　　　　　Washington, DC 20033
Web site: http://www.adoptionattorneys.org

The AAAA is a national association of attorneys who have distinguished themselves in the field of adoption law. The AAAA works to promote reform in adoption law and to publicize information on ethical adoption practices.

American Bar Association (ABA)—Center on Children and the Law
Phone: 312–988–5522
Address: 541 N. Fairbanks Court
　　　　　Chicago, IL 60611
Web site: http://www.abanet.org/child/home.html
E-mail: ctrchildlaw@abanet.org

This program of the ABA Young Lawyers Division provides technical assistance, training, and research programs addressing a broad spectrum of law and court-related topics affecting children.

Dave Thomas Center for Adoption Law—Capital University Law School
Phone: 614–236–6730
Address: 303 East Broad Street
　　　　　Columbus, OH 43215–3200
Web site: http://www.law.capital.edu/adoption/index.htm
E-mail: adoption@law.capital.edu

The Dave Thomas Center seeks to ease and facilitate the adoption process through education, advocacy, and research. The center provides services to families, social workers, lawyers, judges, and others involved in the adoption process.

The Hague Adoption Standards Project
Phone: 703–671–0700
Address: Acton Burnell, Inc.
      1500 N. Beauregard Street, Suite 210
      Alexandria, VA 22311–1715
Web site: http://www.hagueregs.org

Acton Burnell, Inc. has the contract from the federal government to draft regulations for the Intercountry Adoption Act of 2000. The final draft regulations and public comment are available on their Web site prior to publication in the Federal Register.

National Association of Counsel for Children (NACC)
Phone: 888–828–NACC
Address: 1825 Marion Street, Suite 340
      Denver, CO 80218
Web site: http://www.naccchildlaw.org
E-mail: advocate@NACCchildlaw.org

The NACC is dedicated to the representation and protection of children in the legal system. The association provides training and technical assistance to child advocates and works to improve the child welfare, juvenile justice, and private custody systems.

The Special Ed Advocate (Wright's Law)
Phone: 804–257–0857
Address: PO Box 1008
      Deltaville, VA 23043
Web site: http://www.wrightslaw.com
E-mail: pwright@wrightslaw.com

Pete and Pam Wright offer advocacy and legal services and information to people affected by disabilities. Their Web site, publications, and newsletters are excellent resources for parents, advocates, educators, and attorneys.

Appendix B: Literature for Children and Young Adults

❊ PRESCHOOL

Cosby, E.T. (2000). *"A" is for adopted*. Tempe, AZ: SWAK-Pak. *"A" Is for Adopted* is a great bedtime alphabet book that matches each letter to the joys of adoption, such as "I" is for inspiration and "V" is for victory. Each letter is accompanied by a brief poem and a cute, colorful illustration.

D'Antonio, N. (1997). *Our baby from China: An adoption story*. Morton Grove, IL: Albert Whitman. *Our Baby from China* tells the true adoption story of Ariela Xiangwei. The journey is accompanied by actual photos of the people and places involved in the process.

Durrant, J. (1999). *Never never never will she stop loving you*. St. George, UT: JoBiz. *Never Never Never Will She Stop Loving You* shares the story of Annie, a young birth mother who realized adoption was best for her child. The story helps adoptive children understand that they were, and are still, loved by their birth mothers.

Keller, H. (1991). *Horace*. New York: Mulberry. *Horace* tells of a leopard son adopted by tiger parents. Horace loves his family, but he wonders if he really belongs, so he runs away. When his parents find him, Horace realizes they are truly a family despite their differences.

Koh, F.M. (2000). *A China adoption story: Mommy, why do we look different?* Minneapolis, MN: EastWest. Laura Shu-Mei knows that she is adopted, but she does not really understand why she looks different from her parents. *A China Adoption Story* helps parents sensitively explain the adoption process to their young children.

Lewis, R. (2000). *I love you like crazy cakes.* Boston, MA: Little, Brown. *I Love You Like Crazy Cakes* is based on the experiences of an adoptive single mother uniting with her baby daughter in China. Any adoptive mother will relate to this warm, gentle story.

London, J. (1993). *A koala for Katie: An adoption story.* Morton Grove, IL: Albert Whitman. Katie often thinks about babies and about her adoption. After a trip to the zoo with her parents, Katie pretends to adopt her new stuffed koala bear. She learns that parents love and care for their children in many ways.

Miller, K.A. (1994). *Did my first mother love me?: A story for an adopted child.* Buena Park, CA: Morning Glory. A touching letter from a birth mother, *Did My First Mother Love Me?* helps reassure children who do not understand why their birth mothers would make an adoption plan. The book also contains a section for parents on talking to their children about adoption.

Pellegrini, N. (1991). *Families are different.* New York: Holiday House. Nico, a 5-year-old who was adopted from Korea, begins to feel uncomfortable about her family being different from others. Her mother helps her understand that there are many different kinds of families all held together with love.

Rohde, S. (1999). *Adoption is okay.* Garland, TX: Key to the Heart. With both English and Russian text, *Adoption is Okay* helps children understand the transition from a Russian orphanage to an American family. This book introduces children to the events and the emotions that may come with adoption.

Uhlig, S. (2000). *Things little kids need to know.* Wayne, PA: Our Child. Children often worry about how things will change when their parents adopt another child. *Things Little Kids Need to Know* shows children what an important role they play in welcoming and caring for a new sibling.

✻ ELEMENTARY

Boyd, B. (1993). *When you were born in Korea: A memory book for children adopted from Korea.* St. Paul, MN: Yeong & Yeong. *When You Were Born in Korea* provides children with a great deal of information about Korea and the process that led to their arrival in America. The book shares the importance of birth families, baby's homes, foster families, and related agencies.

Brodzinsky, A.B. (1996). *The mulberry bird: An adoption story, revised.* Indianapolis, IN: Perspectives. *The Mulberry Bird* uses personified birds to offer a compassionate look into issues and events that may lead a birthmother to decide adoption is best for her child. This story provides a look into the minds of birthmothers, adoptive families, and adoptees.

Bunin, C., & Bunin, S. *Is that your sister?: A true story of adoption*. Wayne, PA: Our Child. Catherine, a 6-year-old adoptee, talks about adoption and being a family. *Is That Your Sister?* is perfect for helping children of multiracial families deal with questions about adoption.

Dorow, S. (1997). *When you were born in China: A memory book for children adopted from China*. St. Paul, MN: Yeong & Yeong. *When You Were Born in China* offers children a wealth of information about China and their journey into an American family. This book also emphasizes elements of Chinese heritage and culture.

Hudson, A.E. (2000). *Good morning, Vietnam, Good afternoon, USA: An adoption journal*. Mechanicsburg, PA: Franklin's. *Good Morning, Vietnam, Good Afternoon, USA* is designed as an artistic, handwritten journal describing the journey of Christopher Thien Hudson (Ha Cau Thien) from an orphanage in Vietnam to a family in the United States.

Kroll, V. (1994). *Beginnings: How families come to be*. Morton Grove, IL: Albert Whitman. Six families relate their stories of how they came together in *Beginnings*. Children will see that families form in a variety of ways, but each shares the common thread of love.

Molnar-Fenton, S. (1998). *An Mei's strange and wondrous journey*. New York: DK Ink. *An Mei's Strange and Wondrous Journey* gently shares the story of a baby girl's adoption from China into an American family. Poetic text and soft pastel images bring the story to life.

Myers, W.D. (1991). *Me, Mop, and the Moondance Kid*. New York: Dell. *Me, Mop, and the Moondance Kid* is a humorous, yet touching story about families and friendship. T.J. and Moondance have recently been adopted, but Mop must find a family before the orphanage closes. Can baseball be the path to her new family?

Peacock, C.A. (2000). *Mommy far, Mommy near: An adoption story*. Morton Grove, IL: Albert Whitman. Elizabeth deals with the sudden understanding that she not only has her mother here, but also a birth mother in China. *Mommy Far, Mommy Near* looks at the confusion and sadness that children may struggle with, as well as the reassurance that they are loved.

Riedler, B. (1999). *It's time to let you know*. Spicewood, TX: Global Relationship Centers. This heartfelt poem from a birth mother to her child reveals the personal love and sacrifice that birth mothers feel when they choose to make an adoption plan. Children will be reassured that they are still loved and remembered.

Rosenberg, M.B. (1984). *Being adopted*. New York: Lothrop, Lee, & Shepard. Real children share their personal experiences in *Being Adopted*, which takes a sensitive, honest look at the joys, struggles, and concerns that older children may experience when adopted into a family with cultural differences.

Schoettle, M. (2000). *W.I.S.E. up powerbook*. Silver Spring, MD: C.A.S.E. The *W.I.S.E. Up Powerbook* is a workbook designed to empower adoptees to deal with the difficult questions asked by friends, teachers, even strangers. The program teaches four strategies: walk away, it's private, share something, and educate.

Turner, A. (1990). *Through moon and stars and night skies*. New York: Charlotte Zolotow. *Through Moon and Stars and Night Skies* is a young boy's telling of his journey across the globe and into a loving family. This book shares the anticipation, anxiety, and joy felt by many international adoptees.

※ ADOLESCENT AND TEEN

Crook, M. (2000). *The face in the mirror: Teenagers and adoption*. Vancouver, BC: Arsenal pub. Written for both teenagers and adults, *The Face in the Mirror* deals with the often controversial issue of adopted teenagers wanting to search for their roots. Information is based on extensive interviews with adoptees, adoptive parents, and birth parents.

Giannetti, C.C. (1999). *Who am I?: And other questions of adopted kids*. New York: Price Stern Sloan. *Who Am I?* offers insight into many of the myths, questions, and concerns of adopted teens. This book is available to affirm and reassure adoptees as they face their unique issues and concerns.

Krementz, J. (1988). *How it feels to be adopted*. New York: Alfred A. Knopf. Nineteen adolescents openly share their feelings, thoughts, and concerns in *How It Feels to Be Adopted*. Parents and adolescents will appreciate the honesty and sensitivity of this book.

Okimoto, J.D. (1990). *Molly by any other name*. New York: Scholastic. This moving story examines the decision of one girl to find out about her birth mother. *Molly by Any Other Name* looks into the thoughts and struggles that accompany a search for one's roots.

References

Adams, M.J. (1990). *Beginning to read: Thinking and learning about print.* Cambridge, MA: MIT Press.

Ainsworth, M.D.S. (1982). Attachment: Retrospect and prospect. In C.M. Parkes & J. Stevenson-Hinde (Eds.), *The place of attachment in human behavior* (pp. 3–30). Hillsdale, NJ: Erlbaum.

Albers, L.H., Johnson, D.E., Hostetter, M.K., Iverson, S., & Miller, L.C. (1997). Health of children adopted from the former Soviet Union and Eastern Europe: Comparison with preadoptive medical records. *The Journal of the American Medical Association, 278*(11), 922–924.

Alperson, M. (2001). *Dim sum, bagels, and grits: A sourcebook for multicultural families.* New York: Farrar, Straus, and Giroux.

Altstein, H., Coster, M., First-Hartling, L., Ford, C., Glasoe, B., Hairston, S., Kasoff, J., & Grier, A.W. (1994). Clinical observations of adult intercountry adoptees and their adoptive parents. *Child Welfare, 73*(3), 261–269.

American Psychiatric Association. (1994). *Diagnostic and Statistical Manual of Mental Disorders* (4th ed.). Washington, DC: Author.

Americans with Disabilities Act of 1990, 42 U.S.C. 12101 et seq.

Ames, E.W., Morison, S.J., Fisher, L., & Chisholm, K. (2000). Some recommendations from a study of Romanian orphans adopted to British Columbia. In T. Tepper, L. Hannon, & D. Sandstrom (Eds.), *International adoption: Challenges and opportunities* (2nd ed., pp. 33–

39). Meadowlands, PA: Parent Network for Post Institutionalized Children.

Aronson, J. (2001). *Overview of health issues and alcohol related disorders in children adopted from abroad.* Available online at http://www. orphandoctor.com/overview.htm.

Aronson, J.E. (1998). Rickets in Chinese children. *Families with Children from China Newsletter, 3,* 34, 36.

Aronson, J.E. (2000). Alcohol related birth defects and international adoption. In T. Tepper, L. Hannon, & D. Sandstrom (Eds.), *International adoption: Challenges and opportunities* (2nd ed., pp. 23–32). Meadowlands, PA: Parent Network for Post Institutionalized Children.

Ayers, A.J. (1979). *Sensory integration and the child.* Los Angeles, CA: Western Psychological Services.

Babb, L.A. (1999). *Ethics in American adoption.* Westport, CT: Bergin & Garvey.

Babb, L.A., & Laws, R. (1997). *Adopting and advocating for the special needs child: A guide for parents and professionals.* Westport, CT: Bergin & Garvey.

Bagley, C. (1993). Chinese adoptees in Britain: A twenty-year follow-up of adjustment and social identity. *International Social Work, 36,* 143–157.

Barkley, R.A. (1993). A new theory of ADHD. *The ADHD Report, 1*(5), 1–4.

Barkley, R.A. (1998). *Attention deficit hyperactivity disorder: A handbook for diagnosis and treatment* (2nd ed.). New York: Guilford Press.

Bascom, B.B., & McKelvey, C.A. (1997). *The complete guide to foreign adoption: What to expect and how to prepare for your new child.* New York: Pocket Books.

Beech, H. (2001). China's lifestyle choice. *Time, 158*(5), 32.

Bernstein, D.K., & Tiegerman-Farber, E. (1997). *Language and communication disorders in children* (4th ed.). Boston, MA: Allyn & Bacon.

Blackorby, J., & Wagner, M. (1996). Longitudinal postschool outcomes of youth with disabilities: Findings from the National Longitudinal Transition Study. *Exceptional Children, 62*(5), 399–413.

Bordwell, M. (1992, September/October). The link between adoption and learning disabilities. *OURS,* pp. 16–19.

Bowlby, J. (1988). *A secure base: Clinical applications of attachment theory.* London: Routledge.

Brodzinsky, D.M. (1990). A stress and coping model of adoption adjustment. In D.M. Brodzinsky & M.D. Schechter (Eds.), *The psychology of adoption* (pp. 3–24). New York: Oxford University Press.

Brodzinsky, D.M., Schechter, M.D., & Henig, R.M. (1992). *Being adopted: The lifelong search for self.* New York: Anchor Books.

References

Brodzinsky, D.M., Singer, L.M., & Braff, A.M. (1984). Children's understanding of adoption. *Child Development, 55*, 869–878.

Brodzinsky, D.M., Smith, D.W., & Brodzinsky, A.B. (1998). *Children's adjustment to adoption: Developmental and clinical issues* (Vol. 38). Thousand Oaks, CA: Sage.

Brodzinsky, D.M., & Steiger, C. (1991). Prevalence of adoptees among special education populations. *Journal of Learning Disabilities, 24*(8), 484–489.

Brown, R. (1975). *A first language: The early stages.* Cambridge, MA: Harvard University Press.

Castellanos, F.X. (1999). The psychobiology of attention-deficit/hyperactivity disorder. In H.C. Quay & A.E. Hogan (Eds.), *Handbook of disruptive behavior disorders* (pp. 179–198). New York: Kluwer Academic/Plenum.

Cermak, S.A. & Daunhauer, L.A. (1997). Sensory processing in the postinstitutionalized child. *The American Journal of Occupational Therapy, 51*(7), 500–507.

Chalfant, J.C., Pysh, M.V., & Moultrie, R. (1979). Teacher assistance teams: A model for within-building problem solving. *Learning Disability Quarterly, 2*, 85–96.

Chisholm, K. (1998). A three-year follow-up of attachment and indiscriminate friendliness in children adopted from Romanian orphanages. *Child Development, 69*, 1092–1106.

Chisholm, K., Carter, M.C., Ames, E.W., & Morison, S.J. (1995). Attachment security and indiscriminately friendly behavior in children adopted from Romanian orphanages. *Development and Psychopathology, 7*, 283–294.

Clark, K., & Shute, N. (2001). The adoption maze. *U.S. News and World Report, 130*(10), 60–69.

Clauss, D., & Baxter, S. (1997). *Post adoption survey of Russian and Eastern European children.* Belen, NM: Rainbow House International.

Cline, F.W. (1992). *Hope for high-risk and rage-filled children: Theory and intrusive therapy.* Evergreen, CO: Evergreen.

Cohen, J.S., & Westhues, A. (1995). A comparison of self-esteem, school achievement, and friends between intercountry adoptees and their siblings. *Early Child Development and Care, 106*, 205–224.

Collier, V.P. (1987). Age and rate of acquisition of second language for academic purposes. *TESOL Quarterly, 21*(4), 617–641.

Collier, V.P. (1989). How long? A synthesis of research on academic achievement in a second language. *TESOL Quarterly, 23*(3), 509–531.

Collier, V.P. (1992). A synthesis of studies examining long-term language minority student data on academic achievement. *Bilingual Research Journal, 16*, 187–212.

Collier, V.P. (1995). Acquiring a second language for school. *Directions in Language and Education, 1*(4), 3–11.

Cradle of Hope. (1998). *Adoptions from eastern European orphanages overwhelmingly successful.* Available online at http://www.cradlehope. org/surv.html.

Cummins, J. (1982). Tests, achievement, and bilingual students. *Focus: National Clearinghouse for Bilingual Education, 9,* 2–7.

Cummins, J. (1996). *Negotiating identities: Education for empowerment in a diverse society.* Ontario, Canada.

Deacon, S.A. (1997). Intercountry adoption and the family life cycle. *The American Journal of Family Therapy, 25*(3), 245–260.

Dellisanti, G. (1994). *Teaching children from complex backgrounds: A manual for teachers.* Seattle, WA: Children's Home Society of Washington's Adoption Resource Center.

Deutsch, C.K., Swanson, J.M., Bruell, J.H., Cantwell, D.P., Weinberg, F., & Baren, M. (1982). Overrepresentation of adoptees in children with the attention deficit disorder. *Behavior Genetics, 12,* 231–238.

Dorfman, K. (1999). Identifying and treating malnutrition. *The Family Focus, 6*(2), 17.

Dorfman, K. (2001). Overcoming malnutrition: Poverty and parasites. *The Family Focus, 7*(1), 1–2.

English, D. (2000). Listening difficulties in children: Central auditory processing disorder. In T. Tepper, L. Hannon, & D. Sandstrom (Eds.), *International adoption: Challenges and opportunities* (2nd ed., pp. 71–76). Meadowlands, PA: Parent Network for Post Institutionalized Children.

Evans, K. (2000). *The lost daughters of China: Abandoned girls, their journey to America, and the search for a missing past.* New York: Tarcher/ Putnam.

Families for Russian and Ukrainian Adoption. (2001). FRUA comments on the Hague. *The Family Focus, 7*(2), 1–2.

Federici, R.S. (1998). *Help for the hopeless child: A guide for families with special discussion for assessing and treating the post-institutionalized child.* Alexandria, VA: Dr. Ronald S. Frederici and Associates.

Federici, R.S. (2000). Understanding the complexities of U.S. and international adoptions. In T. Tepper, L. Hannon, & D. Sandstrom (Eds.), *International adoption: Challenges and opportunities* (2nd ed., pp. 145–164). Meadowlands, PA: Parent Network for Post Institutionalized Children.

French, G. (1986). Intercountry adoption: Helping a young child deal with loss. *Child Welfare, 65*(3), 272–279.

Garcia, S.B., & Ortiz, A.A. (1988). Preventing inappropriate referrals of language minority students to special education. *National Clearinghouse for Bilingual Education New Focus, 5,* 1–12.

Garrett, L. (1997). Plague of alcohol: Russians are drinking more than ever, with deadly results. *Newsday*, A4, A28–29.

Gilman, L. (1992). *The adoption resource book*. New York: HarperCollins.

Gindis, B. (1997). Language-related issues for international adoptees and adoptive families. *The Post*, *13*, 2–7.

Gindis, B. (1998). Navigating uncharted waters: School psychologists working with internationally adopted post-institutionalized children. *Communique*, *27*(2), 20–23.

Gindis, B. (2000). Language-related problems and remediation strategies for internationally adopted orphanage-raised children. In T. Tepper, L. Hannon, & D. Sandstrom (Eds.), *International adoption: Challenges and opportunities* (2nd ed., pp. 89–97). Meadowlands, PA: Parent Network for Post Institutionalized Children.

Greenspan, S.I. (1993). *Playground politics: Understanding the emotional life of your school-age child*. New York: Addison-Wesley.

Groze, V., & Ileana, D. (1996). A follow-up study of adopted children from Romania. *Child and Adolescent Social Work Journal*, *13*(6), 541–565.

Guralnick, M.J. (1997). *The effectiveness of early intervention*. Baltimore, MD: Brookes.

Haradon, G. (2000). Sensory integration therapy and children from deprivational environments. In T. Tepper, L. Hannon, & D. Sandstrom (Eds.), *International adoption: Challenges and opportunities* (2nd ed., pp. 77–87). Meadowlands, PA: Parent Network for Post Institutionalized Children.

Haywood, H.C. (1992). *Bright start: Cognitive curriculum for young children*. Cambridge, MA: Charlesbridge.

Hostetter, M.K., Iverson, S., Dole, K., & Johnson, D. (1989). Unsuspected infectious diseases and other medical diagnoses in the evaluation of internationally adopted children. *Pediatrics*, *83*(4), 559–563.

Hough, S.D. (2000). Risk factors for the speech and language development of children adopted from eastern Europe and the former USSR. In T. Tepper, L. Hannon, & D. Sandstrom (Eds.), *International adoption: Challenges and opportunities* (2nd ed., pp. 99–119). Meadowlands, PA: Parent Network for Post Institutionalized Children.

Huffman, L.C., Mehlinger, S.L., & Kerivan, A.S. (2000). *Risk factors for academic and behavioral problems at the beginning of school*. In The Child Mental Health Foundations and Agencies Network, *A good beginning: Sending America's children to school with the social and emotional competence they need to succeed* (Paper 1). Washington, DC: National Institute of Mental Health.

Hughes, D. (1997). *Facilitating developmental attachment*. Northvale, NJ: Jason Aronson.

Hughes, D.A. (1998). *Building the bonds of attachment: Awakening love in deeply troubled children*. Northvale, NJ: Jason Aronson.

Hughes, D.A. (1999). Adopting children with attachment problems. *Child Welfare, 78*(5), 541–560.

Hughes, D.A. (2000). Parenting a poorly attached child: Understanding and bonding. In T. Tepper, L. Hannon, & D. Sandstrom (Eds.), *International adoption: Challenges and opportunities* (2nd ed., pp. 137–143). Meadowlands, PA: Parent Network for Post Institutionalized Children.

Hynd, G.W., Hern, L., Voeller, K., & Marshall, R. (1991). Neurobiological basis of attention deficit hyperactivity disorder (ADHD). *School Psychology, 20*(2), 174–186.

Immigration and Naturalization Service. (2000). *Statistical reports.* Washington, DC: INS Demographic Statistics Branch.

Improving America's Schools Act. (1994). Title VII, Part E, Section 7501 (8).

Individuals with Disabilities Education Act. (1997). 20 U.S.C., § 1400 et seq.

Intercountry Adoption Act, PL 106–279 et seq. (2000).

James, B. (1994). *Handbook for treatment of attachment-trauma problems in children.* New York: The Free Press.

Jernberg, A. (1979). *Theraplay.* San Francisco, CA: Jossey-Bass.

Jewett Jarratt, C.L. (1994). *Helping children cope with separation and loss* (2nd ed.). Boston, MA: The Harvard Common Press.

Johnson, A.K., Edwards, R.L., & Puwak, H. (1993). Foster care and adoption policy in Romania: Suggestions for international intervention. *Child Welfare, 72*(5), 489–506.

Johnson, D. (2000). Adopting a post-institutionalized child: What are the risks? In T. Tepper, L. Hannon, & D. Sandstrom (Eds.), *International adoption: Challenges and opportunities* (2nd ed., pp. 5–8). Meadowlands, PA: Parent Network for Post Institutionalized Children.

Johnson, D.E., & Hostetter, M. (1997). Post-arrival evaluations: Identifying medical problems common to internationally adopted children. *Adoptive Families, 30*(2), 14–17.

Johnson, D., & Hostetter, M. (2000). Planning for the health needs of your institutionalized child. In T. Tepper, L. Hannon, & D. Sandstrom (Eds.), *International adoption: Challenges and opportunities* (2nd ed., pp. 9–21). Meadowlands, PA: Parent Network for Post Institutionalized Children.

Johnson, D.E., Miller, L.C., Iverson, S., Thomas, W., Franchino, B., Dole, K., Kiernan, M.T., Georgieff, M.K., & Hostetter, M.K. (1992). The health of children adopted from Romania. *The Journal of the American Medical Association, 268*(24), 3446–3450.

Johnson, D., & Traister, M. (2001). *Health status of adopted Chinese or-*

phans on arrival in the U.S. Available online at http://catalog.com /fwcfc/healthdanajohnson.html.

Karen, R. (1998). *Becoming attached: First relationships and how they shape our capacity to love.* New York: Oxford University Press.

Keck, G.C., & Kupecky, R.M. (1995). *Adopting the hurt child: Hope for families with special-needs kids.* Colorado Springs, CO: Pinon Press.

Klatzkin, A. (Ed.). (1999). *A passage to the heart: Writings from families with children from China.* St. Paul, MN: Yeong & Yeong.

Kranowitz, C.S. (1998). *The out-of-sync child: Recognizing and coping with sensory integration dysfunction.* New York: Skylight Press.

Lemer, P.S. (2001). Prioritizing interventions. *The Family Focus, 7*(1), 3.

Lerner, J.W., Lowenthal, B., & Lerner, S.R. (1995). *Attention deficit disorders: Assessment and teaching.* Pacific Grove, CA: Brooks/Cole.

Locke, J. (1993). *The child's path to spoken language.* Cambridge, MA: Harvard University Press.

Luthar, S., & Zigler, E. (1991). Vulnerability and competence: A review of research on resilience in childhood. *American Journal of Orthopsychiatry, 61*, 6–22.

Marcovitch, S., Cesaroni, L., Roberts, W., & Swanson, C. (1995). Romanian adoption: Parents' dreams, nightmares, and realities. *Child Welfare, 74*(5), 993–1017.

Maskew, T. (1999). *Our own: Adopting and parenting the older child.* Longmont, CO: Snowcap Press.

Mattson, S.N., & Riley, E.P. (1997). Neurobehavioral and neuroanatomical effects of heavy prenatal exposure to alcohol. In A. Streissguth & J. Kanter (Eds.), *The challenge of fetal alcohol syndrome: Overcoming secondary disabilities* (pp. 3–14). Seattle, WA: University of Washington Press.

McGuinness, T.M. (2000). Risk and protective factors in children adopted from the former Soviet Union. In T. Tepper, L. Hannon, & D. Sandstrom (Eds.), *International adoption: Challenges and opportunities* (2nd ed., pp. 41–49). Meadowlands, PA: Parent Network for Post Institutionalized Children.

McKinney, J., Montague, M., & Hocutt, A. (1993). Educational assessment of students with attention deficit disorder. *Exceptional Children, 60*, 125–131.

Meese, R.L. (1999). Teaching adopted children with disabilities: What teachers need to know. *Intervention in School and Clinic, 34*(4), 232–235.

Melina, L.R. (1995). Institutionalized children have problems, show progress after adoption. *Adopted Child, 14*(11), 1–4.

Melina, L.R. (1998). *Raising adopted children: Practical reassuring advice for every adoptive parent.* New York: HarperPerennial.

References

Merzenich, M.M., Jenkins, W.M., Johnston, P., Schreiner, C., Miller, S.L., & Tallal, P. (1996). Temporal processing deficits of language-learning impaired children ameliorated by training. *Science, 271,* 77–81.

Miller, L.C., & Hendrie, N.W. (2000). Health of children adopted from China. *Pediatrics, 105*(6), e76.

Morison, S.J., Ames, E.W., & Chisholm, K. (1995). The development of children adopted from Romanian orphanages. *Merill-Palmer Quarterly, 41*(4), 411–430.

National Institutes of Health. (2001). *National Institute of Child Health and Human Development Study of Early Child Care.* Washington, DC: Author.

O'Connor, T.G., & Rutter, M. (2000). Attachment disorder behavior following early severe deprivation: Extension and longitudinal follow-up. *Journal of the American Academy of Child and Adolescent Psychiatry, 39*(6), 703–712.

Ortiz, A.A., & Garcia, S.B. (1988). *A prereferral process for preventing inappropriate referrals of Hispanic students to special education.* Paper presented at the Ethnic and Multicultural Symposia, Dallas, TX (ERIC # ED 298 701, #EC 210 635).

Pearson, C.M. (2001). Internationally adopted children: Issues and challenges. *The ASHA Leader, 6*(19), 4–5, 12–13.

Pertman, A. (2000). *Adoption nation: How the adoption revolution is transforming America.* New York: Basic Books.

Pollak, S.D., Cicchetti, D., Hornung, K., & Reed, A. (2000). Recognizing emotion in faces: Developmental effects of child abuse and neglect. *Developmental Psychology, 36*(5), 679–688.

Price, P. (2000). FRUA's health and development survey. *The Family Focus, 6*(3), 1–3.

Register, C. (1991). *Are those kids yours? American families with children adopted from other countries.* New York: The Free Press.

Reid, R., Maag, J.W., Vasa, S.F., & Wright, S.F. (1994). Who are the children with attention deficit-hyperactivity disorder? A school-based survey. *The Journal of Special Education, 28,* 117–137.

Riccio, C.A., Gonzalez, J.J., & Hynd, G.W. (1994). Attention-deficit hyperactivity disorder (ADHD) and learning disabilities. *Learning Disability Quarterly, 17,* 311–322.

Rivera, C. (1994). Is it real for all kids? *Harvard Educational Review, 64,* 55–75.

Rogan, W.J., Dietrich, K.N., Ware, J.H., Dockery, D.W., Salganik, M., Radcliffe, J., Jones, R.L., Ragan, N.B., Chisolm, J.J., & Rhoads, G.C. (2001). The effect of chelation therapy with succimer on neuropsychological development in children exposed to lead. *The New England Journal of Medicine, 344*(19), 1421–1426.

Rojewski, J.W., & Rojewski, J.L. (2001). *Intercountry adoption from China: Examining cultural heritage and other postadoption issues.* Westport, CT: Bergin & Garvey.

Rosenthal, J.A., & Groze, V.K. (1992). *Special-needs adoption: A study of intact families.* New York: Praeger.

Russian Life. (2001). Facts and figures. *44*(3), 7.

Rutter, M., & The English and Romanian Adoptees (ERA) Study Team. (1998). Developmental catch-up, and deficit, following adoption after severe global early privation. *Journal of Child Psychology and Psychiatry, 39*(4), 465–476.

Ryan, T. (2000). Alcohol related birth defects and language disorders in children. *The Family Focus, 6*(2), 1, 12.

Safran, S.P., & Safran, J.S. (1996). Intervention assistance programs and prereferral teams: Directions for the twenty-first century. *Remedial and Special Education, 17*, 363–369.

Samway, K.D., & McKeon, D. (1999). *Myths and realities: Best practices for language minority students.* Portsmouth, NH: Heinemann.

Schaffer, J., & Lindstrom, C. (1989). *How to raise an adopted child: A guide to help your child flourish from infancy through adolescence.* New York: Copestone Press.

Schell-Frank, D. (2000). Education and the post-institutionalized child: Parents in the driver's seat. In T. Tepper, L. Hannon, & D. Sandstrom (Eds.), *International adoption: Challenges and opportunities* (2nd ed., pp. 51–70). Meadowlands, PA: Parent Network for Post Institutionalized Children.

Schoettle, M. (2000). Making decisions about birth country connections. *The Family Focus, 6*(4), 1–2.

Section 504 of the Vocational Rehabilitation Act of 1973, 29 U.S.C. § 794 et seq.

Shaywitz, S., & Shaywitz, B. (1988). Attention deficit disorder: Current perspectives. In J. Kavanagh & J. Truss (Eds.), *Learning disabilities: Proceedings of the national conference* (pp. 369–567). Parkton, MD: York Press.

Shen, X., Rosen, J.F., Guo, D., & Wu, S. (1996). Childhood lead poisoning in China. *The Science of the Total Environment, 181*, 101–109.

Silver, L.B. (1989). Frequency of adoption of children and adolescents with learning disabilities. *Journal of Learning Disabilities, 22*(5), 325–327.

Simon, R.J., & Altstein, H. (1991). Intercountry adoptions: Experiences of families in the United States. In H. Altstein & R.J. Simon (Eds.), *Intercountry adoption; A multinational perspective* (pp. 24–54). New York: Praeger.

Simon, R.J., & Altstein, H. (2000). *Adoption across borders: Serving the children in transracial and intercountry adoptions.* Lanham, MD: Rowman & Littlefield.

Snow, C.E., Burns, M.S., & Griffin, P. (1998). *Preventing reading difficulties in young children.* Washington, DC: National Academy Press.

Spitz, R. (1945). Hospitalism: An inquiry into the genesis of psychiatric conditions in early childhood. *Psychoanalytic Study of the Child, 1,* 53–74.

Spohr, H.L., Willms, J., & Steinhausen, H.C. (1993). Prenatal alcohol exposure and long-term developmental consequences. *The Lancet, 341,* 907–910.

Steinberg, G., & Hall, B. (2000). *Inside transracial adoption.* Indianapolis, IN: Perspectives Press.

Tallal, P., Miller, S.L., Bedi, G., Byma, G., Wang, X., Nagarajan, S.S., Schreiner, C., Jenkins, W.M., & Merzenich, M.M. (1996). Language comprehension in language-learning impaired children improved with acoustically modified speech. *Science, 271,* 81–84.

Teicher, M.H. (2000, Fall). Wounds that time won't heal: The neurobiology of child abuse. *Cerebrum: The Dana forum on brain science,* 50–67.

Teicher, M.H., Anderson, C.M., Polcari, A., Glod, C.A., Maas, L.C., & Renshaw, P.F. (2000). Functional deficits in basal ganglia of children with attention-deficit/hyperactivity disorder shown with functional magnetic resonance imaging relaxometry. *Nature Medicine, 6(4),* 470–473.

Tessler, R., Gamache, G., & Liu, L. (1999). *West meets east: Americans adopt Chinese children.* Westport, CT: Bergin & Garvey.

Thomas, A., & Chess, S. (1984). Genesis and evolution of behavioral disorders from infancy to early adult life. *American Journal of Psychiatry, 141,* 1.

Tizard, B., & Joseph, A. (1970). Cognitive development of young children in residential care: A study of children aged 24 months. *Journal of Child Psychology & Psychiatry, 11,* 177–186.

Trolley, B.C. (1995). Grief issues and positive aspects associated with international adoption. *Omega, 30(4),* 257–268.

Trolley, B.C., Wallin, J., & Hansen, J. (1995). International adoption: Issues in acknowledgement of adoption and birth culture. *Child and Adolescent Social Work Journal, 12(6),* 465–479.

U.S. Department of Education. (2000). *Twenty-second annual report to Congress on the implementation of the Individuals with Disabilities Education Act.* Washington, DC: Author.

Vygotsky, L. (1978). *Mind in society: The development of higher psychological processes.* Trans. M. Cole, V. John-Steiner, S. Scribner, & E. Souber. Cambridge, MA: Harvard University Press.

Wadsworth, S.J., DeFries, J.C., & Fulker, D.W. (1993). Cognitive abilities of children at 7 and 12 years of age in the Colorado Adoption Project. *Journal of Learning Disabilities, 26*(9), 611–615.

Wardle, F. (1990). Endorsing children's differences: Meeting the needs of adopted minority children. *Young Children, 45*(5), 44–46.

Welch, M. (1989). *Holding time.* New York: Simon & Schuster.

Werner, E., & Smith, R. (1989). *Vulnerable but invincible: A longitudinal study of children and youth.* New York: Adams, Bannister & Cox.

Werner, E., & Smith, R. (1992). *Overcoming the odds: High risk children from birth to adulthood.* Ithaca, NY: Cornell University Press.

Westhues, A., & Cohen, J.S. (1998). Ethnic and racial identity of internationally adopted adolescents and young adults: Some issues in relation to children's rights. *Adoption Quarterly, 1*(4), 33–55.

Yell, M.L. (1998). *The law and special education.* Upper Saddle River, NJ: Prentice-Hall.

Zametkin, A.J., Nordahl, T.E., Gross, M., King, A.C., Semple, W.E., Rumsey, J., Hamburger, S., & Cohen, R.M. (1990). Cerebral glucose metabolism of adults with hyperactivity of childhood onset. *New England Journal of Medicine, 323,* 1361–1364.

Zeanah, C.H. (2000). Disturbances of attachment in young children adopted from institutions. *Developmental and Behavioral Pediatrics, 21*(3), 230–236.

Index

46; intervention, 45–46, 53; skills, 44; tactile defensiveness, 45

Special education, 127–128, 130, 135; assessment, 18, 82, 135, 139, 140, 143–144, 146; assessment, language, 113–115, 146; assessment, nondiscriminatory, 131–132; Child Find, 130–131; disciplinary action, 133–134, 139; due process, 132–133, 136, 146; instruction, 144; Romania, 53; Russia, 26–28; Section 504, 138–140, 146. *See also* Adoption, intercountry; Early intervention; Groze, Victor; IDEA; IEP; Russia

Temperament, 56

Toxins, environmental, 10, 15–16, 21, 24, 34–35, 54, 66, 70

United Nations, 8

University of Minnesota, International Adoption Clinic, 16, 35. *See also* Development; Development, delays; Health

U.S. Department of Education, 127, 138

Visual impairment, 21, 29, 67, 130

Vocational Rehabilitation Act of 1973, 138; Section 504, 138–140, 146

About the Author

RUTH LYN MEESE is Professor of Special Education at Long-wood University in Farmville, Virginia. She is the author of three textbooks and numerous articles on special education. She is also a member of Families for Russian and Ukranian Adoption (FRUA) and the proud parent of a child adopted at age four from Russia.